The Heart of Your Dog

The Heart of Your Dog

How to Create a Deep Lifelong Relationship with Your Dog Using a New Stress-Free Teaching Method

Ed Noyes

The Heart of Your Dog

Published by
Hidden Cove Press
Friendship, Maine
www.hiddencovepress.com

Copyright © 2014 by Hidden Cove Press

ISBN-13: 978-0692263761
ISBN-10: 0692263764

Manufactured in the United States of America

All rights reserved. No part of this book may be reproduced, stored in a retrieval system or transmitted in any form or by any means, electronic, mechanical, photocopying, recording, scanning or otherwise, except as permitted under Sections 107 or 108 of the 1976 United States Copyright Act, without the prior written permission of the Publisher.

The publisher and the author make no representations or warranties with respect to the accuracy or completeness of the contents of this work and specifically disclaim all warranties, including without limitation warranties of fitness for a particular purpose. No warranty may be created or extended by sales or promotional materials. The advice, techniques, and strategies contained herein may not be suitable for every situation. If professional assistance is required, the services of a competent professional person should be sought. Neither the publisher nor the author shall be liable for damages arising herefrom.

Hidden Cove Press is a division of SGD Industries, Inc.

www.heartofyourdog.com
Email: ed@heartofyourdog.com

For James and Ben

...and all the dogs

How to Use this Book

This book will show you how to build a deeply satisfying lifelong relationship with your dog. In it I will help you identify your dog's highest unmet needs. I will show you how to fulfill those needs and better communicate with your dog.

You will also learn how to teach your dog the essential commands your dog should know. The methods I reveal will enhance your dog's happiness and bring you and your dog closer.

The techniques in this book are easy to follow. I promise with a little patience and understanding the relationship you have with your dog will strengthen with every step you take.

The first part of this book describes your dog's unmet needs and why they are they are the key to your dog's heart. I then describe how to teach the essential commands in ways that will create new connections to your dog's heart.

I recommend reading the entire book to understand the concepts. You can then use it as a reference to guide you as you continue to teach your dog.

Additional Free Resources

Please visit **HeartOfYourDog.com** for additional content.

At the website you can also subscribe to my blog:
Your Dog's Heart Blog

We're on Facebook: **facebook.com/heartofyourdog**

Write me at *ed@heartofyourdog.com* with your questions and comments. I look forward to hearing from you!

Contents

Your Dog's Heart 1
Finding the Heart of Your Dog 4
Understanding Dogness 10
Where Dogs and Humans Meet 16
Basic Techniques 39
Housebreaking 45
No and What is it? 51
Jumping on You and Your Guests 54
Come Here and Right Now 58
Separation Anxiety 66
Stay 69
Sit and Lie Down 71
Poor Dog and It's Alright 74
Good Dog Bad Dog 77
Quiet and Speak 82
Walking, Riding, and Adventures 86
Hop Up and Hop Over 91
Look Out and Get 94
Let's Go and Go Ahead 101
Drop It, Pick It Up, Bring It Here, and Get It 103
Upstairs 109
Whispering 112
The Journey 115
Index 119

Your Dog's Heart

There are dozens of books about dogs. You can learn how to select a dog, how to keep your dog healthy, how to housebreak your dog, how to train your dog to be obedient, and how to teach it tricks. There are also books that wax poetically about noble breeds and epic adventures. Fictional dogs like Buck, Rin Tin Tin, and Lassie spark our imaginations. We embrace their higher nature and wish we could bring forth the same courage and intelligence in our dogs. Off screen these dogs aren't the heroic characters they portray. In fact, they aren't much different from your dog. However, unlike your dog, they have been systematically trained to perform amazing tricks on demand for the camera.

Traditional obedience training often treats dogs as little more than soulless automatons. A strict program of carrots and sticks will force almost any dog into whatever routine behavior is desired by the master. This usually results in a dog that's not just physically dependent and behaviorally dependent, but also profoundly mentally dependent. At the extreme, the strictly obedient dog is unable to think and act outside its box. In short, it becomes a robot dog.

It's not difficult to raise a devoted dog. Most dogs, including robot dogs, will offer devotion in exchange for food and a comfortable place to sleep. Yet, dogs are hopeful animals. They will appear content, even when they have valid needs that remain unmet. Understanding these higher needs is the key to unlocking the heart of your dog.

I can show you how to craft a deep relationship with your dog. There are dozens of ways to simultaneously teach your dog, meet its higher needs, and build connections to its heart. I developed these techniques from working with dogs for over thirty years. If you follow the system I describe, your dog will be blessed with what it desires most, your steadfast companionship. Your dog will reciprocate with that and much more.

My secret is showing you how to be the best possible friend and leader to your dog by understanding all of your dog's higher needs and fulfilling them. Fortunately, your dog also wants to understand you and will meet you more than halfway. The commands you'll teach your dog are crucial lines of communication. They keep your dog safe and help your dog follow the rules of your household, but there is more. You'll find that these lessons go far beyond those basics. The teaching methods I show you are also designed to open new connections to your dog's heart and strengthen the bonds that naturally form. As that happens, your dog will be inspired to learn even more on its own and build a vocabulary beyond what you teach. You will learn how to invent new commands that you can teach by building on your dog's experiences and the vocabulary it has already mastered.

Perhaps dogs are incapable of highly imaginative thought, but that doesn't mean your dog has no imagination. It's wrong to think that it only cares about its physiological needs. Your new relationship will uncover and elevate your dog's higher needs and desires. I promise that your dog will be supremely happy, and you'll be rewarded with the unconditional love that only your dog can give.

Finding the Heart of Your Dog

I am inviting you to make a lifelong connection to the heart of your dog. Your dog comes to you offering the same invitation. Your dog has an open heart and is looking to you for the leadership essential to meet all its important needs. If you accept these invitations and follow the techniques I describe, I promise the relationship you have with your dog will grow deeper and more satisfying for both of you.

When you decide to bring a dog into your family, you're making a serious commitment. If you're adopting a puppy, it can mean an obligation for the next twelve to sixteen years. You'll provide food, water, shelter, exercise, medical care, and all the other physiological requirements, but there is much more you'll do to truly care for your dog.

Consider what happens when you bring a child into your family. Beyond the basics, you offer emotional support. You teach your child how to solve problems. You give your child respect and show it how to respect others. If you're a good parent, your child will grow up happy with confidence and self-esteem. You and your family will feel satisfied and fulfilled. Why not desire a similar life for your dog? Only you and your family can make that happen.

With your new dog, the first order of business is to establish the rules of your household. You'll teach various commands and your dog will build a vocabulary. Eventually it will understand and respond to the meanings behind dozens of words and phrases. During this learning process, you'll be sending other messages to your dog. How they are received will determine your relationship. The messages you send go directly to the heart of your dog. They remain there and are difficult to change. Devotion, trust, fear, passivity, respect, and/or confusion are among the many possible outcomes that you intentionally or unintentionally forge.

The methods I explain help you teach much more than the rules of your household. The commands your dog will learn will be valuable devices you'll use every day to guide your dog through its life. As you show the patience and understanding that every dog needs, you'll find your dog is happier and more fulfilled. This will draw your dog closer to you and deepen your relationship.

As you build these lines of communication, you'll discover that your dog is also capable of being an independent learner. If you encourage it, your dog will strive to understand everything it can about you and your world. On its own your dog will listen and successfully attach meaning to important words without your assistance or awareness. You'll learn how to cultivate this learning process and contribute to your dog's vocabulary without using formal lessons or traditional training. This is one aspect of helping your dog feel fulfilled as it becomes a welcomed member of your family.

Dogs are not people. They're not your children. In recent years we've learned that dogs are actually more like infantile wolves. Over centuries of selective breeding, the capacity of puppies to mature into wild wolves has all but vanished. The modern domesticated dog doesn't develop much beyond its puppy-hood.

Raised from birth, a dog pup and a wolf pup will act about the same. Dog pups will show a little more curiosity, but within a matter of a few weeks the wolf pup will veer toward its wild nature and become uncontrollable. Attempts to domesticate wolves from birth have routinely failed. Meanwhile, the puppy dog will eagerly seek acceptance from its human family.

Dogs have adopted many social behaviors and human-like emotions that can easily seduce us into thinking of them as children, however, dogs retain many of the characteristics of wolves. Recognizing and respecting these similarities and differences is crucial to understanding your dog's true nature.

It's my hope that your dog will live a fulfilled life with maximum joy. Sadly, many dogs never come close to experiencing that ideal. Too many lead pitiful lives of neglect and loneliness. Each year millions of puppies, many born in inhumane breeding mills, are purchased by families who are incapable of caring for them. Many families simply don't understand what the requirements are. These dogs are frequently dropped at overcrowded shelters or dumped in the streets to fend for themselves. Either way, their miserable lives usually end badly. With your commitment and my help, your dog's fate will be much brighter.

I avoid using the words *pet* and *owner*. Pets are toys. Dogs are not toys. If you want a pet, get a pet rock. Dogs are living beings, capable of complex thoughts and emotions. They have real feelings. Furthermore, your dog has no concept of one living being possessed by another living being. You'll never be able to teach this owner/owned relationship to your dog. What your dog does understand is belonging to a pack. Think of your dog as a member of your family/pack. Your dog is already thinking that way. When everyone in your family understands this and accepts it, you'll be on the same wavelength with your dog.

Your dog also understands companionship with humans. You don't need to teach that. Your dog is eager to be loyal to you. You should reciprocate and strive to become the best possible companion to your dog. It will pay dividends.

So, let's agree not to think of you as a *dog-owner* with a *pet*. When I use the phrase *your dog*, think of it as a relationship. *Your* is like *your uncle* or *your mother*. Don't think of it in the ownership sense like *your shirt* or *your car*.

So what does that make you? You are the leader. You are a teacher. You are the parent in your family/pack.

I should add a quick word about pronouns. I use *it* a lot. I do this mainly to make the book easier to read. The phrase *he or she* is a little too awkward. I don't think of my dog Chimo as an *it*. She is a she. I hope any dog reading this book won't be offended. (Since Chimo is spayed, *it* may be more appropriate, though.)

Speaking of *it*, removing your dog's sexual needs is a good idea. It not only helps control the canine population, it also removes your dog's impulse to roam. With a content-to-be-at-home dog, it's easier to reach its heart and build the deep relationship I describe.

Fulfilling your dog's higher needs is a journey. Your successes along the way will help your dog live a wonderful life. Your dog's happiness should always be the focus of your efforts. It's my hope that, when you follow this road map, you'll be rewarded with your dog's amazing love and loyalty. It will touch your heart every moment of every day for all the years you're together.

To begin the journey, you must understand what life is like from your dog's perspective. That is the essence of *dogness*.

Understanding Dogness

Years ago when I was studying Human Ecology in college, I was introduced to the concept of anthropocentrism. If you ask anyone to name the most significant species on the planet, most people will instinctively pick humans. Many cultures have used that bias to subordinate all other creatures and satisfy their every extravagance, no matter how harmful. Those beliefs and others like it tend to prevent people from appreciating the way other animals perceive the world. It also undermines the compassion they should feel.

The primary way that all animals understand the world is through their senses. It's how we all navigate the environment from ants to whales. It's difficult for even the most enlightened among us to understand what it's really like to be an ant or a whale. Consequently, it's easy to treat ants, whales, and all animals as nothing more than chattel. In this way the thoughts and feelings of other species become irrelevant.

Some modern religions reinforce this disregard. They teach that the natural world was created so that man can have exclusive dominion over it. Meanwhile, some so-called primitive cultures actually honor the creatures that inhabit their surroundings. In rituals, they even impersonate them, hoping to acquire their special characteristics. Their legends are filled with animal spirits; yet, as people from these cultures join the modern world, they abandon traditional practices in favor of a more rational and materialistic outlook. Their connections to the natural world that were once vital for survival are broken and their ancestral empathy for animals is lost.

In spite of all this, it's still possible to imagine the lives of other creatures. As children, we play-act popular zoo animals — tigers, elephants, and monkeys. Yet, in this game kids only learn about the outward characteristics and not much about the important inner lives of the creatures they imitate. As adults, we can take this game to a deeper level and imagine much more.

UNDERSTANDING DOGNESS

For a moment, consider *antness* and what it truly means to be an ant. Close your eyes and go deep inside their seemingly manic world. Spend a few minutes there. Next time you encounter one scurrying in your path you might stop and think before squishing it with your foot. Pick another to imagine, *elephantness, owlness, fishness, snakeness*. When you get around to *dogness*, spend some serious time. This is an important first step toward understanding the heart of your dog.

If you were to morph into a dog right now, what would you experience?

The first thing you'll notice is that your eyesight, particularly your ability to distinguish colors, is diminished; however, you'll become more aware of things that suddenly move in your line of vision. Your nose is now bombarded with thousands of new scents. At first you may be confused, but soon you're able to sort through the onslaught and distinguish subtle differences, much the way you did with your color vision, as a human. Hearing is acute, too. You face another challenge to prioritize all the sounds you now hear. As you get used to your new powers, you realize that you can now detect how close or far away sounds and scents are. You also notice that previously putrid and repulsive odors aren't so bad anymore. In fact, some are downright pleasing. As you explore this new world, your nose, eyes, and ears are hanging close to the ground. You scratch and dig to acquire and process hidden information about what's below the surface. You find you can diagnose where other animals have trekked. You can even estimate how recently they've passed, based on your ability to detect the freshness of their scent. You're probably excited by the sight or smell of a squirrel, rabbit, or raccoon. Chasing, attacking, and killing are irresistible; then you discover that you can now run much faster than any human. You also notice that you're comfortably warm, since normal canine body temperature is 101°F. If you aren't already part of a family or pack, you're constantly on the lookout for one to join or start. Fortunately, you do have a loving family, so you mark your territory. All this romping has left you a little tired. You go home to take a nap. After a quick slurp of water, you settle down and instantly fall asleep. Suddenly you jump up wide-awake, startled by an unexpected sound. You determine it's nothing important, so you fall back to sleep just as quickly. Sleeping thirteen hours a day feels just about right.

Now morph back to human form and consider canine intelligence. Unfortunately, *dumb dog* is a common expression. It's easy to insult your dog when its behavior doesn't match your expectations. Yes, compared to humans, your dog's IQ is much lower. That isn't only because your dog has less total brain power. The truth is, your brain and your dog's brain are wired differently. Higher

UNDERSTANDING DOGNESS

The Gray Wolf (*canis lupus*) is the sole ancestor of your dog.

Gray Wolf, (voor de natuur, Saxifraga) by Jan Nijendijk / CC BY-SA 3.0 (the color image was converted to alpha)

level thinking and planning aren't important for your dog's survival. What's more important is the ability to rapidly process and analyze the huge volume of sensory information to make quick decisions.

Wolves need to have sharp wits and respond instantly to everything they confront. Dogs have similar instincts. Humans, on the other hand, rely on complicated layers of reasoning that filter multiple options before reaching a decision. Without human intervention, dogs will rely on their impulses. To survive as a dog, you need to act fast. If you hesitate, that squirrel will get away.

All these things and more require a particular intellect unfamiliar to humans. Is it fair to measure canine intelligence based on human standards? Dogs are not dumb. The channels in their brains are simply different than ours.

In spite of these differences, there are many ways in which dogness and humanness overlap.

Where Dogs and Humans Meet

As puppies, dogs are playful, easily imprinted, and eager to belong to your family/pack. Successful membership requires that they have the ability to establish friendly relationships, along with a desire to conform to your rules.

From the earliest times, dogs that could read humans and understand human emotions were selected for breeding. The genes that expressed this ability were passed on through successive generations. The result is a closeness between the emotional lives of dogs and humans. Consider the personality traits that we share.

Love

Jealousy

Affection

Appreciation

Anger

Forgiveness

Regret

Hatred

Passivity

Domination

Kindness

Curiosity

Courage

Sorrow

Loyalty

Tenderness

Joy

Playfulness

This is hardly an exhaustive list. Some qualities are controversial, such as regret. Also, not all dogs demonstrate every trait, just as they are not all manifest in every human. In general, though, they regularly appear in both dog and human populations. Can you name another animal capable of this many human emotions? This explains why dogs have found a special place in the modern family.

Eye contact is an important way that your dog tunes-in to your emotions and reads you. For most animals, staring is a sign of aggression. If you stare into a wolf's eyes, you'll be inviting trouble. Dogs haven't entirely lost this instinct to feel threatened. If you ever get into a confrontation with a dog, even with your own dog, you can escalate the encounter with your eyes.

If your dog is especially protective of its food dish, try this experiment. First, pick a time when your dog is hovering over its dish. Stand perfectly still at a safe distance and get your dog's attention. Look it straight in the eyes without any expression on your face, then look at its dish. Look back at your dog's eyes. Keep going back and forth. Notice how your dog reacts.

For most dogs, aggressive eye contact is the exception. More often your dog will welcome what you may call a staring contest. Even though its eyes seem to be fixed on your eyes, your dog is actually looking for subtleties in your facial expression.

Your dog expresses emotions with tail wagging, barking, and physical movements. Compared to humans, its face is expressionless. Your body movements, along with your voice, also express your emotions; however, most day-to-day expressions happen with your face. Your dog will usually understand what your physical movements mean and will understand a number of spoken words, but the big *tell* for your dog is found in your face. If your dog was more wolf-like and threatened by eye contact, it wouldn't have the ability to understand so much about you.

The importance of your facial expression is easily understood in everyday communications. The same words in a phone call and in an email can be interpreted differently; however, when we're face-to-face, the meanings are clearest.

Because dogs are not threatened by eye contact, they've developed a knack for reading faces. Correctly construing human emotions and intents must have been a favored trait for which dogs were selectively bred.

You can use this canine talent to help build a better relationship with your dog. Three things need to happen:

1. You need to give your dog access to your emotions by frequently engaging with it and using eye contact.

2. You need to be consistent and not send conflicting messages. Don't do anything that might confuse your dog.

3. You need to encourage successes. When your dog correctly reacts to your expressions, it needs positive reinforcement.

Encouraging success can't be accomplished in a lesson. It happens when it happens. The first step is to simply do more staring. Sometimes your dog will stare simply because it wants something and needs your attention to make it happen. It could be about food, water, or a bathroom break. You should be aware of those situations and respond appropriately. That's one form of encouragement; however, when your dog is reading you, that's an even better opportunity to offer encouragement.

Let's say your dog just woke up from a nap and is checking in with you by looking into your eyes. Reciprocate by staring back and maintaining that connection for a few seconds, then try flashing a sincere grin. If your dog wags its tail, hurray! You'll know it correctly read your face. Give it a big hug along with a good dog. Try to spot more random opportunities like this to reinforce your dog's reading skills.

Whenever I think about *dogness*, I find myself envious of the amazing abilities of dogs to smell and hear things beyond the range of humans. We would all love to have those canine talents, yet which human features would dogs want? Maybe they have a deep enough appreciation to desire our special intellect. Perhaps they would like to have our ability for language and speech. Well, there's one human feature I'm certain every dog would love to have — arms and hands with articulating fingers. Imagine your dog being able to scratch any part of its body and easily pluck out those nasty ticks; no more struggling to grip bones. It would be so easy to grab things to smell and eat like the squirrel that didn't get away. Those itchy ears would be a thing of the past.

Our hands are important to dogs. How often have you been minding your own business and your dog nudges your hand with its nose? It's telling you to scratch, pat, and pay attention.

Chimps are considered to be much more intelligent than dogs, yet they have no clue when it comes to hand signals. Dogs understand pointing and gesturing. Professional trainers often rely on dozens of complex hand signals to give directions. As you'll see, there are several circumstances where basic pointing is a useful technique for you and your dog.

Unfortunately, there are times when hands can create problems for dogs. If you've ever been to a shelter and met dogs that have been severely abused by people, you've probably noticed some of the sad consequences. A dog beaten into submission will cower if you try to touch it with your hands. Meanwhile, a dog that has fought against cruelty will try to bite your fingers. When a dog is beaten with a stick or some other instrument, the dog doesn't blame the stick. It knows that the person and the hand behind the stick are responsible. These mistreated dogs require special handling to recover from their trauma. The good news is that even though it takes time, abused dogs usually respond well. When they do accept human contact again, they often become fantastic companions. The message is simple — never strike your dog with your hands. Correction: Never strike your dog, period.

In his classic *Call of the Wild*, Jack London describes a sled team commanded by an aggressive alpha-male dog. The other dogs, including Buck the hero, form a more or less linear hierarchy of submissive followers. In the story, the alpha-male keeps the pack members in check and enforces the role of each dog, resorting to violence when necessary. London's story bolsters a popular myth about the way wolf and dog packs behave.

Until recently, it was believed that wolf packs were always ruled by a powerful alpha-male that subdued the rest of the pack with regular dominance behaviors, such as mounting and pinning. The alpha-male's reign lasts until another wolf gains enough strength to initiate a credible challenge. According to the narrative, a savage fight ensues. If the old alpha wins, he retains his position. If he loses, the challenger becomes the new alpha.

It's interesting that many parallels to this alpha-male model can be found in many human settings like in sports, warfare, and business, where intimidation can be a decisive factor. This behavior is also observed in other primate groups, such as chimp communities, where alpha-male leadership is chosen by domination over the other males. While many other factors are important in human and chimp social order, it's easy to see how we've projected our patterns of behavior when making assumptions about the way wolf packs are organized. New evidence offers a different explanation of social order in wolf packs.

The new research has found that wild wolf packs are more like families. The alpha wolf is actually similar to a parent figure, leading a cooperative pack. Leadership is acquired by consent from family relationships and not from aggressive dominance and submission behaviors. As a wolf pup grows up and reaches the age of two or three, it often leaves the pack anyway to find and pair with a wolf of the opposite sex to start a new pack.

Today, many trainers still rely on strategies based on the alpha myth. While dominance and submission is observed among dogs, using that as a training technique can have unintended consequences. A submissive dog can be forced to comply, yet it can also lose the confidence fundamental to its happiness. It's also been discovered that excessive human dominance can backfire and provoke aggressive behavior in otherwise tame and cooperative dogs. It's not worth the risks. Besides, do you want your dog conditioned to calculate its family relationships based on who is dominating whom? There are more important matters you'll want your dog to think about.

Knowing that wolf packs behave like families is good news because it suggests a better way to work with your dog to establish a deeper relationship. Just as you engage with your children and guide them through life, you can use the same strategies with your dog. If your children see you as an overly aggressive and domineering parent, you may get them to obey in the moment, but in the long run your children are more apt to grow up resentful, troubled, and possibly defiant. The path to your dog's happiness is not unlike the path you follow to raise happy kids.

When your dog is welcomed into your family/pack aggressive intimidation by you is unwarranted. Instead, you should gently assert your role as the parent/leader. Done properly, your dog will happily accept this relationship and quickly discover its appropriate role in the family/pack.

It's important that each family member negotiates a similar relationship with your dog. At first your dog might try to bully a weaker family member, particularly a young child. If safety becomes an issue, you'll have to intercede, yet it's far better for each family member to independently assert and establish a friendly relationship with your dog. Doing that early on is much more effective, and it will leave a more lasting impression on your dog. If you always have to scold your dog when it's bullying one of your children, imagine what goes on when you're not around. It's rare, but bad things do happen when an aggressive bully-dog mixes with a defenseless small child. Those tragedies can be easily avoided.

Dogs want to belong. Teaching how your household works and how you expect it to fit in is an important priority for your new dog. It's right up there with housebreaking.

As you read about the techniques I recommend, you won't see me use the term *obedience training*. Most parents won't use obedience training to describe how they raise their children. Some believe that these terms are acceptable for dogs because they're naturally dumb and can't socialize with humans without being forced to obey. These trainers believe you must become the alpha, or your dog's *master* (another word I don't use). If it's wrong to use these words to describe your relationship with your children, it should be wrong for dogs, too. This isn't about political correctness, it's about the mentality you bring to your role in your family/pack.

If you want to reach your dog's heart, you need to think as a parent/leader, not as a master. It's not the words themselves that are harmful. When your dog hears them, they don't register one way or another. Instead, I'm suggesting that you get them out of your head because they're inconsistent with the deep relationship I'm advocating.

Make no mistake, dogs and human children are not the same. You value your children above all others. In every respect there are significant differences between dogs and children; however, it's safe to say that in several ways dogs are child-like. Consequently there are many parallels that inspire some helpful techniques for guiding your dog's behavior.

When you become a responsible parent/ leader in your family, you're naturally protective and nurturing. You don't impose your will unnecessarily. You're the leader by consent. When your dog accepts your leadership, you should reciprocate by doing everything you can to fulfill your dog's needs.

In 1943, Abraham Maslow published his famous paper, *A Theory of Human Motivation*. His *Hierarchy of Needs* is often represented by a pyramid with the most basic needs at the bottom. Figure 1 on the next page is a diagram showing one popular version of Maslow's theory. I prepared a new pyramid representing a *Hierarchy of Canine Familiaris Needs* (Figure 2). Take a moment to compare it to Maslow's version.

In the two pyramids, the physiological and safety needs of humans and dogs are almost

WHERE DOGS AND HUMANS MEET

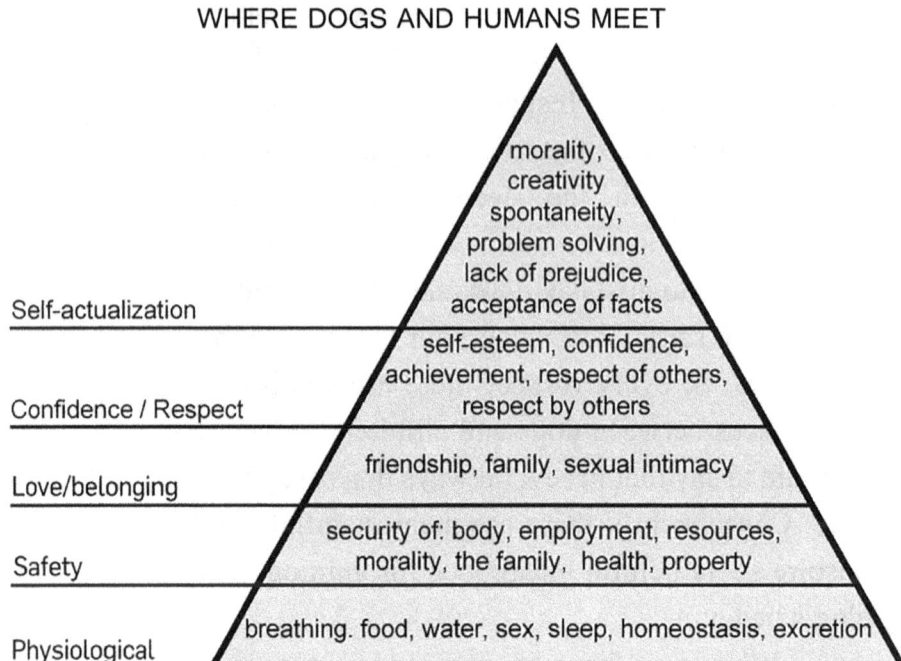

Figure 1: Abraham Maslow's *Hierarchy of Needs*, 1943. Derived from "An interpretation of Maslow's hierarchy of needs" by J. Finkelstein / CC BY

identical. Assuming your dog is fixed, sex is eliminated as a consideration.

Morality, employment, resources, and possessions don't apply to dogs.

Your dog's toys could be called possessions, but they're hardly needs in the sense that possessions are important to humans. In its place I put territory. Your dog needs space and will mark ownership of its territory. It will feel threatened when a strange dog or other animal invades its territory. It will instinctively attempt to defend the space. Having a secure territory helps satisfy your dog's need to feel safe.

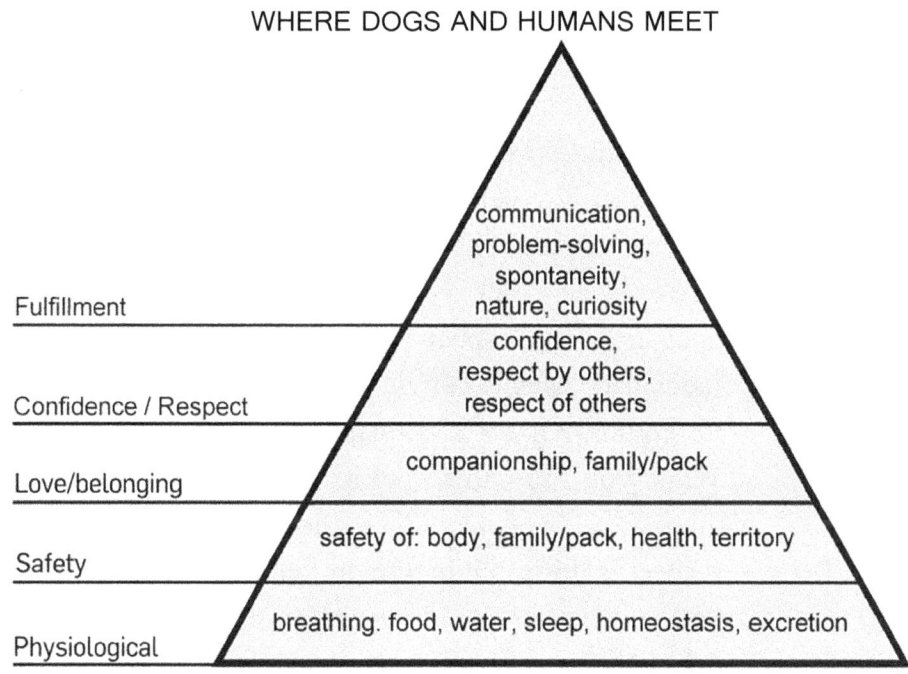

Figure 2: *Hierarchy of Canine Familiaris Needs*, 2014.

In a sense, work dogs have employment, but it's a stretch to equate it to human employment. Work imposed by humans doesn't pass for what can be called a canine need.

Once these physiological and safety needs are met, you should address the other needs that are close to your dog's heart and higher up the pyramid. We can equate love, companionship, and family/pack to the human need for friendship and love. Your dog naturally craves your love and is eager to establish a lifelong bond with you. Reciprocating that love should be an obligation you enthusiastically accept when you bring a dog into your home.

Self-esteem isn't associated with dogs. Dogs are not vain, so our concept of the need to be respected is of no concern to your dog; however, to reach your dog's heart, you'll still need to show respect for your dog's position in the world. Specifically you should respect its role in the family/pack and respect its personal space. When you show this kind of respect, your dog is guaranteed to respect you in the same way. Mutual respect is desirable in human relations and should be equally desirable in your relationship with your dog. Ideally, it is a cornerstone of all relationships. With mutual respect you and your dog will have more opportunities to engage on a common plane and widen the channels of communication. It's hard to imagine how you can reach your dog's heart without mutual respect.

As long as household rules are followed, your dog needs the confidence to assert itself like any other family member. Your dog should have the freedom to show its personality and try new things. You shouldn't arbitrarily suppress quirky canine behavior. A dog lacking confidence will be difficult to reach.

Self-awareness in dogs is a controversial topic. Cynics believe that dog behavior is little more than involuntary responses to stimulus. They point to Ivan Pavlov's 1901 conditioned reflex experiments. Pavlov was able to use a buzzer to trick dogs into drooling after repeatedly sounding it prior to mealtime. Since I salivate in anticipation of a delicious meal, too, I have to reject Pavlov's conclusions about reflexive dog behavior.

People who have spent years working with dogs and observing them in a wide variety of situations will attest to their thinking ability. For example, there's no doubt in my mind that dogs dream. I don't have laboratory data to back up that conclusion, yet every dog I've known from time to time while napping will move its legs, often with muffled yelps, as if to be running and chasing. If this is evidence of dreaming, isn't more implied? We know that dreaming is an activity of the subconscious. Does the existence of a subconscious in your dog tell us that your dog must also be *self*-conscious and thus self-aware? No one knows for sure but put me in the camp with those who say, Yes!

MRI examinations have shown that the same regions in dog brains and in human brains are activated when experiencing similar emotions. Evidence like this is mounting, and it supports my belief that dogs are genuinely astute and knowing animals.

For all that I am advocating, the final conclusion of the scientific community doesn't matter much. We know that your dog has an emotional heart. That's sufficient for me. I simply want to show you how to reach it. Unlocking your dog's intellectual potential, whatever it may be, is just a part of that process. In Maslow's *Hierarchy of Needs*, self-awareness is a prerequisite for self-actualization. In my *Hierarchy of Canine Familiaris Needs*, I decided to straddle this canine self-awareness/self-actualization debate for the time being. Instead, I suggest a broad category that I call Fulfillment to better represent your dog's highest needs. Within that category are five important needs: nature, curiosity, spontaneity, problem-solving, and communication.

Nature

Humans have created civil societies and vast artificial landscapes to enhance our survival. We rearrange the chaos of nature and battle entropy to make the world fit our purposes. Those things provide the context in which we seek our self-actualization. Dogs are less interested in civil society and artificial landscapes.

When we contemplate unspoiled nature, we discover beauty and inspiration. Too often we also see it as something that needs changing. Your dog is attracted to nature in a different way. It sees a potential home. It's happy to flow through nature as it exists. Improvements are unnecessary.

If your dog is unhappy and then allowed its freedom, it may decide to slip away and seek a wild pack of feral dogs to join. Family dogs, and particularly those living in an urban landscape, have an unmet need to be in nature. Your dog yearns to experience more than the hum-drum of kitchens and manicured yards.

Once your dog has fully bonded to you and your family/pack, and you're confident it won't run away when it's off leash, you should provide as many experiences in nature as possible. Take your dog with you on hiking and camping trips. Let your dog become the animal it was designed to be. Its senses will be liberated and overwhelmed by all the new smells and sounds. Your dog will love it. It needs that experience. Imagine if you were forced to wear glasses that filtered out all but one or two colors. You would never be able to experience the fullness of the world or the fullness of your human potential. How can your dog feel fulfilled, if it's isolated from the incredible assortment of sensory experiences to be had in nature? When you give your dog the freedom to be in nature, as often as you can, you'll be touching your dog's heart.

Curiosity

Curiosity is an important way that puppies learn. Unless your puppy gets into something dangerous or it egregiously violates a household rule, curiosity should be encouraged and rewarded. To a puppy, everything is new, so everything inspires curiosity. By the time your dog is two or three, the home environment is adequately cataloged and curiosity diminishes.

It's possible to create new waves of curiosity by exposing your dog to new people and places. Taking your dog for rides is one way. Opening the window to let in refreshing scents will enhance the journey. In cold weather your dog will probably stick its nose to the vent, if the settings are for outside air. Time spent alone in a parked car does nothing. Whenever possible, let your dog out for a short walk to inspect what's around. A boring landscape of small patches of grass, scrawny trees, and dumpsters isn't exactly a romp in the woods, but it's sure to reveal hundreds of new scents that your dog will find worthy of exploration.

Spontaneity

Spontaneity is easy for dogs, since they don't do a lot of planning. However, too often spontaneity atrophies when life becomes a constant routine. You can liven things up by being more spontaneous yourself. Dogs quickly adapt to routines. Your dog probably recognizes the jingle of your car keys and knows what that means. Your dog has observed how you get up at the same time each morning and proceed through a predictable routine before running off to work. Maybe your dog follows you around noticing everything you do step-by-step; boring.

Why not mix it up? Do something unpredictable. Fall down on the floor and start playing with your dog for a minute or two. Run around the house and try to get your dog excited. Your dog will probably think you're crazy at first. Make it a plan to do this on a random basis, maybe two or three times a week. Your dog will pick up on it and anticipate that a surprise may be in the works. Hopefully your dog will even try to provoke your surprise behavior. When this happens, reward your dog with a special crazy act.

There are plenty of games like this that your dog will love to play and initiate spontaneously. You may also find your dog creating original variations. Invent as many opportunities for your dog to be spontaneous as you can. It's too easy for your dog to fall into a rut. Don't let that happen.

Problem Solving

Work dogs spend a significant part of their lives solving problems. They're trained to analyze situations and perform the correct services to produce the expected results. Rescue dogs, police dogs, drug sniffing dogs, guide dogs, and herding dogs confront new challenges every day. In most cases they relish the opportunity to resolve the issue and serve their human companions.

The family dog has far fewer problems to solve. That doesn't mean your dog wouldn't benefit from an occasional challenge. Create a game that will incorporate your dog's special skills and have some fun at the same time. Grab one of your dog's favorite toys. Maybe it's a tennis ball. Preferably it's something slobbered over, so it will be easily recognized. Call your dog over and show the object. Use it to tease your dog for a few seconds. Cover its eyes, then have someone quietly hide the toy somewhere in the room. Let your dog go and watch the wild search begin. After a few successful searches, your dog may even invent a strategy. You can then add an extra challenge that might trick your dog at first. Hide the toy in the same place on successive searches until your dog immediately goes to that one place again and again. Once you're sure your dog will go there the next time, hide it someplace completely different. How quickly it solves the problem isn't as important as your dog's enjoyment of the challenge. Most breeds will love this game. Some breeds won't. My experience with huskies, for example, is that they're apathetic to tennis balls, Frisbees, and most toys. Your experience with huskies may be different.

Communication

Communication is the ultimate fulfillment need for you and your dog. If you can't express things to your dog in a way that your dog understands, your dog will be less motivated to connect with you. Likewise, when your dog does try to communicate and you don't respond appropriately, your dog is apt to become discouraged and apathetic about the prospects for communication.

Think about your human parenting. If you and your children can't communicate, unhappy outcomes are sure to follow. For any dog, a complete failure to communicate can result in serious behavioral problems. Too often it becomes a deal breaker for the dog's membership in the family. A sad goodbye trip to the local shelter might be the final result.

The good news is that dogs have an incredible ability to understand human language. Some super-dogs have been taught over 300 words. Your dog only needs to learn twenty to thirty words and phrases to connect with you and have a deep relationship. Pay attention though because your dog probably won't stop with only what you choose to teach.

My dog Chimo has learned many words on her own. For example, I have two sons, eleven and twelve, who are always coming and going. They have responsibilities around the house, and it's not unusual for them to be upstairs making it necessary for me to yell their names for one reason or another. Chimo has quietly observed all this and noticed who appears when a name is called. One day Chimo, needing a bathroom break, nudged my hand. It was James' turn to walk her, so I said, "Go see James," not expecting any response. She listened attentively, then proceeded to trot over to James and start nudging him.

Chimo is always tuned in to conversations, scanning the words and deciphering the language to find out what's going on. I know there are dozens of other words and phrases that she's picked up through simple associations. I'm sure when she hears me tell my boys to "go brush your teeth," she knows what will happen next, even though it doesn't involve her. It would be tough to test this particular bit of knowledge, but since she independently learned their names, there must be much more that she understands.

What follows are my specific techniques and commands that will help you better communicate with your dog. The particular words you use aren't important, so feel free to use whatever you like, as long as you're consistent. Some of the commands are built on sounds used in other commands. Keep that in mind before you deviate from what I use. The order in which you teach them isn't important either. Every combination of dog and household is a little different, so some commands may be more relevant to your situation than others.

It's my hope you'll use what follows to build a lifelong relationship that will fulfill your dog's special needs and bring to you all the companionship and happiness that your dog has to offer.

Basic Techniques

From the perspective of most dogs, humans are giants. When you make eye contact, you're usually looking down at your dog. In wolf society (and most societies), relative position is one way that dominance can be imposed. Once you establish your parental rank in the family/pack and your dog has accepted its role, there's no need to be overbearing. In fact, you should think about re-balancing your relationship. When teaching so much about proper behavior to a small puppy, an imbalance is inevitable, regardless of best intentions. Good communication can't take place if one party feels dominated and submissive.

BASIC TECHNIQUES

You can begin the re-balancing process by getting down on the floor and making friendly contact with your dog. That may not be practical considering the breed and your particular household situation. The objective is to get on an even level with your dog and look straight into its face. Make it a positive experience. Hugging and ear scratching combined with soothing words will help your dog become relaxed and ready.

In most cases your dog will welcome this face-to-face attention. If not, be patient. Back off and try again later when the atmosphere is more conducive.

When getting close to your dog in situations like this, cheek-to-cheek seems to be a particularly good way to show affection and to

BASIC TECHNIQUES

bond. Hold your dog's head loosely near the neck with hands on each side just behind the ears. If your dog is relaxed, you'll be able to gently move its head around without a struggle. Dogs love having their ears rubbed and scratched. Don't be too rough, though. Another area you can scratch while holding your dog close to you is its chin and throat.

You may laugh or think it odd, but licking is a great way to show special affection. Before you call me crazy, let me explain. You've probably seen a video or pictures of a mother giving birth to pups or perhaps you've witnessed it first-hand. One of the first things the mother does is lick her babies. Seeing puppies being born in person gave

BASIC TECHNIQUES

me the idea to use licking to imprint a loving parental relationship on my dogs from the moment I adopted them. Make no mistake, I never actually lick my dogs. Yuck! Instead, I make a licking and slurping sound as I rub the top of their head and hold my face close to their's. I swear it works and, as funny as all this sounds, you should try it, too.

Another way to show your willingness to treat your dog as an equal member of the family is to put your head under its head in a playful way. You might find that your dog will respond by immediately trying to nuzzle under your head to show submission. Affection and praise will let your dog know that this is just a game and that you don't feel threatened by relative positions.

There are stairs in our house, and I often find Chimo lounging at the top. When I see her there, I crawl up in a crouched position. When I get close to her, I nuzzle my head beneath hers and a competition ensues to see who can get under whom.

Mastering close face-to-face contact is important. It comes into play when you're teaching your dog how to follow your household rules. It also can be used in any situation where you need to get your dog's attention.

When you follow this technique, it should always be non-threatening. You want your dog to pay attention, but also welcome the connection

BASIC TECHNIQUES

while being relaxed and receptive.

You shouldn't use this to yell at your dog. Don't think of it in the same way that getting in someone's face is meant in human relations. So, before you use this technique for teaching, make sure that everyone is calm and that your dog is receptive.

If you have a domineering dog, you need to correct the relationship before going face-to-face. Correct your dog in the same firm but gentle way you would handle an unruly small child. Any doubts about your role as the parent/leader need to be settled as a prerequisite to everything that follows.

Using treats to teach your dog is unnecessary. Treats do work, but it's better if your dog isn't motivated by food to follow the rules of the family/pack. Treats take the focus off you and the lines of communication you're trying to establish. If your dog can't smell something good, you'll run the risk that your dog will ignore you. Hugs, affection, and praise are all that you need.

It's nice to give your dog a treat from time to time, but not as a bribe. Treats should be free or part of a game and not used as a tool for behavior modification. I do use treats in a game that introduces and teaches a few commands. In this situation the treat isn't a reward for obeying the command. I'll explain how that works later.

If you have a good relationship, your dog

BASIC TECHNIQUES

will always want to please you. It's unnecessary to use the carrot and stick method. Dogs don't need harsh punishment. In fact, they rarely need any punishment at all. Instead, establish a solid line of communication and your dog will usually follow your instructions to the best of its ability. When you use this face-to-face technique, always top it off with positive reinforcement in the form of praise and affection, even if your purpose is to correct poor behavior.

Doing things this way is a big improvement over the corporal punishment often inflicted by choke collars and all those gadgets that administer shocks. The peaceful climate you'll create is ideal for teaching. It's also much better for your nerves and for your dog's peace of mind. This is how you open the paths that you'll explore to reach your dog's heart.

Housebreaking

One of the first things you'll work on with a new puppy is housebreaking. There are dozens of ways to teach your dog to take its business outdoors. You should consider all the advice you hear and pick whatever makes sense for your situation.

Over the years I've tried just about every method. By far the best I've found is crate training. Housebreaking is always difficult when you have to leave your dog home alone before it's ready. With any method, the more bathroom breaks you can give your dog, the better. If you decide to use a crate, position it to help your dog make that mad dash outside when you get home.

Inevitably there will be mistakes. Mistakes always create stress. I don't mean stress in your dog; I mean stress in you! When a mistake happens, probably your immediate impulse is to explode on your dog. You're upset, and you're certainly justified for feeling angry. Unfortunately, your dog sees it differently. Your dog is just doing what comes natural. Instead of resorting to fireworks, get your dog outside quickly so you and your dog can calm down and relax. Romp a bit and lavish praise on your dog when it does a follow-up in an appropriate location. Give the praise using the face-to-face technique to emphasize the positive behavior and to help keep perspective on the technique when you use it again for an opposite message during the lesson.

When you come back into the house happy and relaxed the lesson can begin. Typically dogs have short memories when it comes to breaking rules. In most situations, if you wait too long to deliver a corrective lesson, your dog won't be able to connect it to its improper behavior. A mistake on the floor is an exception to that rule. Your dog will remember what it did, so taking some time outside won't cause any confusion when it's time for the lesson. In fact, taking a few minutes to make sure you and your dog are relaxed will help it focus.

First, hold your dog nearby and point to the

mistake. Next, get face-to-face. Get extra close so that your nose is on your dog's nose and your eyes are only inches away. Speak in a clear, serious, non-playful, yet non-threatening tone. Talk to your dog using the **No** command while pointing to the mess. There's no need to be harsh. If your pup struggles to get free, you'll want to be a little more firm than you typically are with other lessons, but if the pup gets too excited and you've lost its attention, it's best to let it go and wait for the next opportunity to deliver the message. Chances are your dog already senses your displeasure and understands what it's about.

Don't ever stick your dog's nose in it. Your dog can smell it just fine from any distance in the house. Your dog won't find the odor offensive anyway, so there's no reason to resort to this outdated and cruel practice.

When you get through the lesson (ten to fifteen seconds should be enough time), top it off with a little affection without praise. Don't go overboard with the affection, though. You don't want to undermine the lecture. Leave your puppy alone for a minute or two to let the message sink in. Be sure to immediately clean up the mess while the puppy watches. You can keep saying **No** in a firm voice to reinforce the lesson. Always do a thorough job to remove as much scent as possible.

I've never encountered a dog that can't be house trained. Mistakes only happen under two circumstances:

1. Your puppy's muscles are too weak and can't hold it in. Don't worry. A healthy pup will outgrow that.
2. Your dog doesn't yet understand the rule. When your dog learns the rule, it will be followed.

A lack of desire to be a good citizen in the family/pack isn't at issue. Don't ever think your dog is bad or evil if it doesn't catch on right away. Stay relaxed. You should have no worries. If you get discouraged, remember these three tips:

1. Remain calm and patient with your puppy.
2. Give plenty of bathroom breaks.
3. Try to do a better job teaching.

Above all, don't blame your dog, conclude it's stupid, or resort to hitting. Be confident that your dog will get through this phase.

Another reason I like the crate method is that after your dog is housebroken you can use it as a cave for your dog. If you leave the crate open, your dog will probably hang out and take naps there on its own. That behavior should be encouraged. If your dog is comfortable going in and out on its own, it will be easier to confine your dog in the crate when it's time for you to leave, while your dog isn't housebroken.

HOUSEBREAKING

In the wild, wolves need shelter. A natural cave is an ideal spot for them. It provides protection from the elements and a place to hide from predators. A cold climate dog will dig a snow cave to sleep and stay warm at night. You may find that your dog will gravitate to similar cave-like places in your home — under a table, under a bed, or between a chair and the wall. If you make the crate a comfortable place, it will become a personal sanctuary for your dog.

After housebreaking, place the crate out of the way, but close to where the family congregates. Alternatively, if your dog sleeps in your room, keep it near your bed. You can experiment with locations to find an ideal spot where your dog is most comfortable.

When there's too much commotion, your dog will often retreat to the security of its cave to escape the chaos.

There are many good crates on the market. Chimo uses the Petnation 614. It sells for under $50 on Amazon.com. It's made of canvas and can be easily folded for moving. It comes in different sizes. The largest is only eleven pounds. I endorse it because I like it and Chimo likes it.

Chimo's cave sits between the couch and the wall in our living room. I've even put a board on top of it with a small bookcase above so it doesn't take up useful space. We leave it unzipped so she can use it whenever she feels like it.

When you're home, it's probably a good idea to limit your dog's access to certain rooms during housebreaking so you can keep an eye out. When you're confident that your dog understands the rule, you can gradually open more rooms to allow more freedom. Just be sure to watch your dog when it roams. The far corners of your home may become equivalent to the outdoors in your dog's mind. If a mistake happens, a little more instruction will be necessary. Mistakes like this just mean that your dog misunderstood and thought that you only wanted your immediate family area kept clean. Consider it a blip and not a back-to-the-drawing-board crisis.

If you follow these methods during housebreaking, you'll get the job done and you'll be strengthening the channels of communication that will help you, as you teach more commands to your dog.

Also, when you provide a sanctuary cave for your dog you'll be showing respect for your dog's space, which will help your dog become a confident and happy member of your family/pack.

No and What is it?

During housebreaking there will be plenty of opportunities to use the **No** command. **No** is a great universal concept that your dog will need to understand early on. It will be learned quickly. There are many other rules specific to your household that you can begin to teach using **No**.

If you catch your dog in the act of chewing a slipper, you should be happy because this is a perfect opportunity to teach a rule. Go face-to-face and nose-to-nose while you remove the slipper. Say **No** several times slowly with a slight pause between each **No**. Do it in a calm but firm voice, then offer your dog a chew toy and show some affection when it's accepted. Five to ten seconds is all it takes. Don't get angry; communicate. Make sure the slipper is kept out of sight and out of reach so there is no confusion or temptation. Explaining things as you would to a child is a little too complex for your dog to grasp. **No** by itself will do the job fine. If you yell or come down too hard, your dog will think that chewing anything is unacceptable. That's why you want to substitute the chew toy immediately and praise your dog when it chomps on it.

It won't take long for your dog to catch on. Unless there's a major distraction, hearing **No** will usually be enough to stop your dog in its tracks.

Before you impulsively use **No** over and over to control your dog's every behavior, carefully consider what rules are important and what rules are not so important. Chewing furniture, getting into the garbage, peeing on the floor are appropriate times to use **No**. Please keep in mind that the first year or two of your dog's life are peak periods for exploration. Smothering your dog with too much negativity could inhibit curiosity. Try distracting your dog or physically moving it away from a situation where a rule is about to be violated. You'll have plenty of time to teach all the rules.

To keep things balanced, it's a great time to introduce a new term to your dog's vocabulary: **What is it?** When you notice your dog transfixed on something new like a butterfly, say **What is it?** with a playful and inquisitive voice. The idea is to encourage your dog to explore further. As long as the object is harmless, keep egging your dog along. When the curiosity is satisfied, reward your dog with some happy affection while you repeat **What is it?** In our language it doesn't make sense to use **What is it?** after the fact. To a child you would probably ask *what was that?* with a different tone. With your dog it's better to keep it simple even if it doesn't make literal sense to you. Your dog will understand it as a combination of *time to do some investigating* and *investigation well done*. You can adjust your tone between the two uses, if you like.

Once it's learned, you can apply this command to different situations whenever you want to alert your dog to something. It could be a noise that was unnoticed, or maybe you want to point your dog's attention to an insect for fun. Dogs are swamped with hundreds of sounds and smells. They also have a tremendous ability to sort through the clutter. **What is it?** is a great way to focus your dog's mind onto something it skipped over.

Let's say a stranger is approaching your door. Maybe you want your dog to bark or growl. **What is it?** is a handy expression that will get the job done. Hopefully that situation won't happen often, but if it does, you'll be glad your dog understands.

Jumping on You and Your Guests

Used correctly, **No** is an effective way to stop and calm an excitable dog that is acting up. One common behavior that's particularly aggravating is the habit of jumping on you as a greeting. When this happens it's important to stay calm. Above all you don't want your dog to misinterpret your meaning.

When you come home after an extended separation, your dog is going to be excited and happy to see you. Jumping on you is an offering of love and a desire to reconnect. Don't reject those emotions. Not only will you confuse your dog, but you may also damage the connections to your

JUMPING ON YOU AND YOUR GUESTS

dog's heart that you're working to build.

When you come home tired, the last thing you want to deal with is a yelping, jumping dog. Teaching a rule against this behavior takes a little time and effort. Done properly it pays dividends.

The first step is to be prepared before you open the door. Don't walk in with your hands full of stuff. You'll need to have your hands free. Wait to bring groceries or other items into the house. Leave them in the car for a few minutes.

When your dog jumps, put your hand out palm first in your dog's face with a gentle but firm **No** combined with **Down**. That should drop your dog to the floor for at least a second or two. Seize that opportunity to get down on the floor, too. That will eliminate the need for your dog to jump again. Reassure your dog with affection that you're happy to be reunited. After a moment or two use a toy or point to something away from you to distract your dog. When your dog has calmed down and the greeting is complete, get back on your feet and go about your business.

Chances are your dog will start jumping on you again. Repeat the palm gesture and **No Down** commands. This time don't drop to the floor and don't give affection. You've already reassured your dog that you're not rejecting it, so now you can be more firm.

Eventually your dog will catch on that the **No Down** is for jumping and doesn't mean *No*.

I hate you. As it begins to sink in, stop using **No** and stick with **Down**. That will clarify **Down** as a distinct command.

Every member of your family needs to use the same technique. At first your dog might think that the rule only applies to jumping on you. The rule you want to teach is *no jumping on humans*. Each member of your family needs to practice the **Down** command. Consistency is essential.

The real test happens when guests arrive. Ideally, your guests will be on board with your strategy and ready to help with the same lesson. Unfortunately, your guests will probably have a hard time appreciating how important this is, especially if they don't have dogs of their own. Try to explain it anyway. They don't need to get on the floor to reassure your dog. In fact, it's probably better if your dog's feelings are hurt. After all, your guests aren't part of the family/pack. Who cares about the bonds between your dog and them? It's your relationship with your dog that matters.

The worst thing that can happen is when your guests immediately show affection to your dog in response to the jumping greeting. Your guests are nice people. Even if they dislike your dog jumping on them, they probably don't want to offend you by scolding your dog. "Oh, what a cute dog" and "I don't mind" are often heard in this situation. The point is that *you* mind. If your guests allow your dog to jump on them, it

JUMPING ON YOU AND YOUR GUESTS

creates a no-win situation for you. If you have to intervene and use the **Down** command, your dog will probably think you're being selfish.

Dogs understand jealousy. Newborn pups compete with the rest of the litter for their mother's attention. They never lose that impulse and will often compete within the family/pack. Your dog assumes that you're pushing it out of the way to get to your guests first. Your dog thinks you want to jump on your guests, too! Ideally, your guests will reject your dog and thereby take the onus of jealousy off you. If your guests really want to engage with your dog, ask them to wait until your dog has calmed down and everyone is settled.

If your guests aren't dog lovers and your dog is too social, you may need an alternate approach. Have a family member take your dog to a different part of the house away from your guests and distract it with some play time. If that doesn't work, you may need to temporarily confine your dog while your guests are visiting. Be prepared for some whimpering and barking that may need correction.

If it doesn't seem to be working right away, don't resort to harsher measures out of desperation. Above all, don't cave and let your dog slobber over your guests. Stick with this calm and deliberate approach. This behavior almost always improves with age, so be patient.

Come Here and Right Now

You'll often need to round up your family/pack. Your dog must respect the **Come Here** command without hesitation. Imagine a situation where your dog is about to run into traffic, step onto thin ice, or face some other hazard. **Come Here** can't be a suggestion.

Before you start teaching **Come Here** make sure your dog knows its name. You don't want to confuse things. The name you pick should be used to get attention and nothing more. If your dog comes when you call its name, that's fine. It should happen only because your dog is interested in what's going on and volunteers to come to you, not because it's an order to appear before you. One way to reinforce this is to use your dog's name before most, if not all, of your commands. That will wash out any particular meaning other than *Attention!*

You can teach **Come Here** in a two part lesson. Start by practicing indoors in a quiet room. Pick a room that doesn't have an easy path for your dog to escape. Use a leash. Make sure everyone is calm. Position your dog a few feet away. Say **Come Here** and pat your knee or chest or side. Keep it upbeat. Act excited. If your dog responds, lavish praise. If your dog doesn't respond and just gives you a silly look, gently tug on the leash and repeat the command. If that doesn't work, pick your dog up and bring it to you. Don't drag your dog with the leash. Hold your dog close to you and repeat the command three times. Each time you say **Come Here**, hug and relax to simulate pulling your dog closer. Return your dog to the starting position and repeat the steps. There's no need to go face-to-face during this part of the lesson.

A five minute lesson twice a day for a few days should be enough for your dog to understand the meaning. As your dog gets the hang of it, drop the leash onto the floor before you say the command. Eventually you should get results with no leash.

Only use those words during the lesson. Don't experiment with the command when your dog is romping around elsewhere. Finally, when your dog responds consistently without the aid of a leash, you'll be ready for part two.

So far your dog only knows one meaning for **Come Here**. Dogs are territory conscious, so your dog might think it only applies to the room where the lesson took place. This is similar to a problem you may have encountered during housebreaking, if your dog assumed keeping things clean only applied to certain parts of the house.

Wait until your dog is busy romping in a room where you can easily make a capture. Say the **Come Here** command. If there are other people or dogs around use your dog's name first to get its attention. If necessary, repeat **Come Here**, but only once. If your dog promptly responds, go crazy with praise and affection. Get excited. If there's no response, pick up your dog and take it to where you spoke the command. Now is the time to use the face-to-face technique with some mild affection. Repeat the command a few times while holding your dog; no excitement, no parade. Reserve the party for occasions when you get an instant response. Don't scold your dog either. You don't want your dog to associate **Come Here** with a bad experience. This part of the lesson needs to be done indoors where you can capture your dog. Make sure you have 100% compliance with the **Come Here** command before taking the next step of teaching it outside.

When you're ready to work outside you should begin with a leash, just as you did inside. Go back to the technique you used in the first part of the lesson and follow all the steps. It should go quickly, since all you're teaching now is that **Come Here** applies everywhere.

There's nothing more embarrassing than a dog that runs around and won't come when called. Saying the **Come Here** command over and over again is pointless. In fact, it's counterproductive. Your dog hears you, but makes the choice to not respond. If this happens, it's important that you become the enforcer. You have to grab your dog. Chasing an unwilling dog is also an exasperating experience. If your dog is deliberately avoiding you and can't be caught easily, it's unwise to continue the pursuit. Your dog is probably enjoying the chasing game and thrilled by the power it has over you. If there's no danger present, it's best to ignore the situation and wait for your dog to return on its own.

When your dog does return, stay calm. Don't yell or inflict punishment. It will have the opposite effect. Your dog will only associate the punishment with returning and associate a fun game with running off. Instead go back to the beginning and calmly teach **Come Here** all over again indoors with a leash.

As a responsible parent/leader to your dog, you cannot let it off leash outside unless you're

100% confident that your dog will respond to the **Come Here** command 100% of the time and under all circumstances. Since most people have difficulty teaching this command, we have leash laws that must be followed.

How soon you can trust your dog to honor this vital command may also depend on the breed of your dog and its particular disposition. There can be great variation. Some independent-minded breeds generally find it difficult to follow the command. Other less excitable breeds are more willing.

How well your dog responds to **Come Here** is a true test of the relationship you've built. Mutual respect is important. Don't get discouraged and, above all, don't get angry with your dog. Keep working at it. The effort will help strengthen the connections you're building to reach the heart of your dog.

Once you've made **Come Here** an absolute command there are some exceptions you should consider.

To this point, you should be delivering **Come Here** in a firm no-fooling-around tone; however, there are situations where your judgment about the importance of **Come Here** could be unwarranted in the mind of your dog. Your dog may want to overrule you. Before you call me a hypocrite, consider the following situation.

You're walking your dog. It just pooped.

You're eager to get back home, so you issue the **Come Here** command. What if your dog needs to do more? An absolutely obedient robot dog will comply and you'll feel proud of your ability to control it. That's fine until a few hours later when your dog can't stand it and has gone all over the carpet. If your dog somehow holds it in, that isn't good either. Why make your dog miserable? Better yet, allow your dog to communicate to you; *wait a sec. I need a little more time.* I think you would be okay with that.

First, you need to be solid with the meaning of **Come Here**. Start a new lesson by varying the tone. In the bathroom break situation use a soft tone, say it once, stand still, and wait. Your dog should get the cue that you're not apt to instantly yank the leash or start chasing. If your dog is done, it will come to you. If it's not done, it will linger. What if your dog doesn't come and nothing more happens? Maybe your dog just wants to finish sniffing something. Within reason that should be okay with you, too. Make it a negotiable situation, but don't make it an invitation to defy your wishes on a whim. Regardless as to what happens, you need to work it so you're teaching a variation that your dog will associate with the proper meaning.

Granting variations to **Come Here** can be risky. You could undermine the importance of the command, if your dog doesn't catch on to the subtleties. There's a solution for that, too. It's the

Right Now modifier. In addition to introducing tonal variations, add **Right Now** to **Come Here** when it's an absolute command. You can run through the original lessons for **Come Here** using **Come Here Right Now** in its place. Be sure to insert a slight pause between the two phrases so your dog will understand that the combination means you're being insistent. Also, use more face-to-face, as you begin to teach **Right Now**.

Don't teach the original **Come Here** lesson with **Come Here Right Now**; otherwise, **Right Now** won't have any special meaning. Keep **Right Now** in reserve for times when you really need it.

In practice, if your dog responds to **Come Here**, hold your fire. Only use **Right Now** when your dog doesn't respond. It should convey *I really mean it and you'll be sorry if you don't get over here immediately*. Be ready to enforce it when you use it.

Even if your dog understands the tonal differences and performs well with **Come Here** alone, it's a good idea to add **Right Now** to your dog's vocabulary. If your dog understands **Right Now** as a modifier, you'll be able to use it with other commands when some extra emphasis or urgency might help.

Another word of caution is necessary. Don't overuse **Right Now** or it will quickly lose its meaning. Tonal differences and **Right Now** are ways to grant (and deny) your dog the option to negotiate over the mighty **Come Here** command. With success, you'll be challenging your dog to make decisions and solve problems. You'll also be building your dog's confidence while practicing mutual respect.

Separation Anxiety

Dogs, like wolves, depend on their packs. Your dog relies on you as the parent/leader for everything, food, water, shelter, and all the other needs from physiological to fulfillment. When left home alone, your dog is apt to feel abandoned. Panic is a natural response. Your dog might scratch on doors in an attempt to get out and follow you. It might also bark and howl to call you back. If you don't return, your dog might even get a bit psychotic and decide to rip, chew, and tear whatever is nearby. In short, it will misbehave in ways it would not, if you were home.

If you teach your dog, as a pup, to remain

content by itself, most of this can be avoided. Start by leaving your dog alone in the house for a few seconds. This won't give your dog enough time to misbehave. When you walk back in, reward your dog with reassuring praise and affection. Wait awhile and repeat. Do that a few times, then leave for a slightly longer period. When you feel your dog is tolerating the separation, try driving away. Your dog will hear your car and know what that means. At first take your car out of the driveway, turn it around and come back. Eventually you'll be able to have longer absences without problems.

It's a good idea to mix things up even after your dog has done well at being alone for hours. If you're like me, it's not unusual to forget something and return home after a minute or two on the road. When your dog observes this pattern, or more correctly, this broken pattern, your dog will relax with the thought you may be back any moment. Of course, by now your dog realizes that you always come back no matter how long it takes. It will soon accept its role as a special guardian of the home territory.

When you leave, don't make it a fussy goodbye. There's no need to heighten the stress of separation by making a point of it. Simply ignore your dog and depart casually. With this strategy you'll be keeping things calm and helping your dog relax while you're away. If you fuss over your dog before you leave, you'll send a signal that the separation will be a terrible experience. If you simply walk away without acknowledging your dog, you'll communicate that the separation is no big deal.

If you're someone who plans to take your dog everywhere, you might want to rethink that idea. A well-behaved dog that can be left alone without panicking is a happy dog.

If you think you're depriving your dog of your company, weigh that against how your dog feels about being cooped up in your car. Sooner or later every dog must face being alone for some period of time.

Separation anxiety can be distressing to your dog. You should cure your dog of this syndrome while it's young. A dog that's accustomed to being alone with a minimum of stress is also a more confident dog.

Stay

Stay is another important command. Most dogs want to be in the middle of everything, but there are times when it's better for your dog to be in a particular spot. **Stay** is the flip side of **Come Here**. Ideally you'll have **Come Here** well understood before attempting this lesson. **Stay** is easy to teach.

Sit your dog down and give it a little attention. Slowly back away one step at a time. Say **Stay** with each step and hold your hand out with your palm toward your dog's face, like a police officer directing traffic to stop. At first, go a short distance, then call your dog using **Come Here**.

If your dog performs both commands correctly, lavish it with praise and affection. Repeat the steps until your dog has the hang of it.

Once your dog knows what to do and what not to do, increase the separation bit by bit. Eventually you should be able to go into other rooms and wait longer and longer before summoning your dog. If your dog gets impatient and breaks out of position before you call, return to a shorter time and distance challenge that your dog has already mastered. If your dog is having difficulty you can deliver the initial **Stay** command in face-to-face mode.

Teaching **Stay** in small increments helps keep things calm. Your dog will be more attentive, too.

By now you and your dog should be in a happy zone of relaxed teaching and eager learning.

Sit and Lie Down

Most people will teach their dogs **Sit** and **Lie Down** early on. Either command can be used to help your dog calm down when there's too much excitement. They're fairly simple to teach. It's just a matter of putting the dog in the desired position and repeating the command. You should teach these commands separately so your dog doesn't **Lie Down** in anticipation when you say **Sit**.

First teach **Sit**. When that's understood, teach **Lie Down**. Your dog may interpret them as a sequence anyway, concluding that **Lie Down** is just more **Sit**. It makes sense to think of it that

SIT AND LIE DOWN

way. To your dog **Sit** means *put my butt on the floor* and **Lie Down** means *put my butt and belly on the floor*. You'll know that **Lie Down** equals more **Sit** to your dog when you say **Sit** while your dog is already lying on the floor. If it gives you a confused look, your dog is probably thinking *my butt is already on the floor*.

You can teach your dog to have a more precise understanding of the two commands. Simply say **Sit** while forcing your dog up when it's lying. I've taught this to a few of my dogs, but have since abandoned it. It has little practical value for me or my dog, so I put it in the category of a trick. Why would you need your dog to assume a sitting position, if your dog is comfortably lying down?

Poor Dog and It's Alright

This combination of commands is among my favorite. When you use them correctly, you'll be making a direct connection to your dog's heart.

Let's say you stand up from your chair and you don't notice that your dog is lying on the floor next to you. You accidentally step on a tail or a foot. Your dog yelps, startled more than hurt.

This is a great opportunity that shouldn't be wasted. Immediately go to the body part that was hurt and make a big fuss; and I do mean a big fuss. Go way beyond what the situation requires. Rub the imaginary wound and say **Poor**

Dog (substitute your dog's name for **Dog**) over and over again in a sad tearful voice. Repeat this sympathy routine every time a situation like this pops up. Also, use **Poor Dog** any time your dog is obviously feeling distressed in any way.

You accomplish three things with the **Poor Dog** command. First, you've demonstrated that you'll always come to the aid of your dog. It's hard for a dog to communicate when it's in pain. You always want it to look to you for help, comfort, and sympathy. Second, you'll be making a significant emotional connection. Finally, you're introducing a useful phrase to your dog's vocabulary. When your dog is sad or has had a rough experience, you can now say **Poor Dog** to show empathy and respect. The only way your dog will know what that means is if you teach it by excessively fussing over every real or imagined injury.

Here's an illustration of just how impactful this can be. Many times my dogs have been romping around in chilly weather and found themselves cold and wet. I'll approach them making eye contact. The moment I say **Poor Dog** they begin shivering. I can assume they're thinking something like *If he says I'm hurt by this cold feeling, I must really be hurt*. With one of my dogs, it got to the point where I could make him shiver in almost any circumstance by simply uttering **Poor Dog** in a sad sympathetic tone. (Is this an example of self-awareness?)

After a few **Poor Dog** commands, provide your reassurance and affection with **It's Alright**. Try to associate **Poor Dog** with the sympathetic observation of distress, and associate **It's Alright** with the comforting affection. By maintaining this subtle distinction you can use **It's Alright** by itself at other times when you simply want to reassure your dog or give a little boost to its confidence to go ahead with something.

Adding these phrases to your dog's vocabulary can also be helpful when your dog experiences a frightening sight or sound. If your dog is scared by thunder, fireworks, distant gunshots, or sirens, you can do a better job of comforting your dog with **It's Alright**. If you can communicate that it shouldn't worry, you'll be taking another giant step closer to the heart of your dog.

Good Dog Bad Dog

You should always be looking for ways to say **Good Dog** and avoid having to say **Bad Dog**. Without any particular reason you should be constantly reminding your dog that it's a **Good Dog**. Your dog is a **Good Dog** just by being itself. It's a great confidence builder. Chimo hears it dozens of times each day in my normal chatter. The ratio of **Good Dog** to **Bad Dog** should be about 1,000 to 1.

Your dog will learn these words quickly when you associate them with reward and punishment. Punishment should be a tiny part of your relationship. If you follow the face-to-

face eye-to-eye technique, it's hard to imagine a situation where punishment is ever necessary, yet even in the best of circumstances, sooner or later a situation will arise and your dog will learn what **Bad Dog** means.

Experts debate whether or not dogs are capable of feeling shame and regret. We've all seen dogs cower when scolded for bad behavior. Are we projecting the human attribute of regret on our dogs and giving them credit for feelings they don't really have? Those who believe that dogs are incapable of shame and regret point to cowering as a response in anticipation of punishment.

The way to escape the severe negativity associated with **Bad Dog** is to create two versions based on the tone of your voice. This is similar to how you developed tonal differences for **Come Here**.

First, there's the harsh **Bad Dog**, which you'll use when you're showing extreme disappointment. Yes, you'll hurt your dog's feelings. Your dog will remember your anger. The experience will probably help your dog do better next time, whether it feels regret or not. **Bad Dog** requires a recovery and reconciliation period during which you'll forgive your dog, and your dog will forgive you. The **Bad Dog** experience creates a mild trauma in your relationship, so try to avoid it in the first place. There are usually better ways of handing the situation. It's my hope that the harsh **Bad Dog** will be so rare in your relationship that your dog will forget its meaning and adopt an alternate understanding when it hears those words.

The good news is that you can easily mend any lingering resentment from the harsh **Bad Dog**. One way to do that is by introducing a soft version of **Bad Dog**.

I taught this to Chimo by tossing biscuits. The rule is, if Chimo catches it in mid-air, she gets praise and can trot off to enjoy her prize. On the other hand, if she misses, she's not allowed to grab it off the floor. I pick it up and I toss it again until she successfully catches it.

After we worked out the rules and practiced the routine for a while I started saying **Bad Dog** when the biscuit dropped to the floor and **Good Dog** when she caught it. Chimo knows that letting the biscuit drop to the floor isn't really all that bad. I certainly don't think of Chimo as a truly **Bad Dog** in the harsh sense when that happens. Chimo also knows that she always gets the biscuit at the end of the game, no matter how many tries it takes. Using **Bad Dog** this way morphs its meaning into something like this: *I've made a mistake, which I'm about to correct. Soon, I'll become a good dog.* Contrast that with the harsh **Bad Dog** where the intent is to be hurtful.

If your dog adopts the *about to become a good dog* meaning for **Bad Dog**, you'll be encouraging your dog to focus on turning **Bad Dog** into **Good Dog**, regardless of the situation. It will be less apt to feel dejected, or worse, to become fearful of you. To your dog, **Bad Dog** can mean either a bottomless pit or a stepping stone. I prefer a stepping stone.

These days when Chimo hears the soft **Bad**

Dog she understands the meaning and actually wags her tail. It's an opportunity and not a sentence.

With regular use the everyday **Good Dog** morphs a bit, too. **Good Dog** should be the normal, happy, healthy condition of your dog and a routine affirmation. It doesn't need to be reserved for high praise.

Your dog understands the tone of your voice and your level of excitement. Your dog will know when it is receiving special recognition. As you talk to your dog, you will add words that convey your special happiness and appreciation, not realizing your dog is understanding some of the literal meanings. Your dog will sense your enthusiasm and actually make correct associations to words it hears over and over. In this way you informally add to your dogs vocabulary. You are teaching without explicit commands and proper lessons, yet to your dog it is just as valid as your work with formal commands. Creating more and more lines of communication is the best way to reach your dog's heart.

This also demonstrates that even with a negative phrase like **Bad Dog** you can find ways to show respect and encourage confidence, which can build even more connections to your dog's heart.

Quiet and Speak

Dogs bark. That's a fact of life. For centuries people have been trying to interpret the meaning behind dog barks. Some barks are clearly the aggressive warnings from a dog standing its ground. Other barks are demands for attention. Whatever the specific meaning, barks, growls, yelps, and whimpers are usually emotional outbursts. They are an important means of expression.

In your family/pack you'll need to teach your dog that incessant barking is inappropriate. There are gadgets that will give your dog an electric shock whenever it barks. They work, but

QUIET AND SPEAK

at a high cost to the relationship you should be building with your dog. No matter how mild the shock, these devices are unnecessary. There is a better solution.

As soon as you hear an undesired bark, hold your dog's mouth shut and give it a gentle squeeze. Be careful not to hurt your dog. Give it a second to move its tongue inside its mouth so it won't get pinched by its teeth. You want to convey to your dog that you're closing its mouth and holding it there to gain your dog's attention and stop its ability to bark. Next go eye-to-eye and softly but firmly say **Quiet**. Repeat the command a few times and let go. Follow up, if necessary.

Saying it softly helps convey your message by example that we all need to dial down. Yelling **Quiet** at your dog is like barking and will send conflicting messages. Quieting down the room helps, too. Turn down the music, TV, and conversations while the message is being delivered to your dog. If the rest of the family/pack continues being loud, your dog will feel it should have the right to be loud, too.

If there's something that always triggers unnecessary barking, such as the doorbell, bring your dog over to the source. Have someone ring the bell over and over while you admonish your dog with **Quiet**. The idea here is to flood your dog with the sound to the point that it loses its significance and no longer requires a response.

QUIET AND SPEAK

The impulse to bark will subside.

Don't go overboard with **Quiet**. You should allow your dog to bark and growl from time to time to sound off. You don't want to suppress its emotions to the point where your dog becomes passive and apathetic, or worse, becomes resentful. **Quiet** needs to fit in with the other reasonable rules.

One way to balance the need to bark is to teach your dog to bark on command. Besides expanding its vocabulary, when you ask your dog to **Speak**, you're encouraging your dog to express itself.

It can be a slow process to teach **Speak**. Get your dog's attention and tap the side of its mouth. Imitate your dogs bark and say **Speak**. Keep repeating this until your dog gets the idea or is so annoyed that it growls or barks. When this happens, however softly at first, get excited with plenty of praise and affection. A good time to practice this is when your dog is already a little hyper. Don't try to teach **Speak** if you told your dog to be **Quiet** moments ago. It will probably take several sessions for your dog to catch on. Be sure to practice the command regularly to strengthen the meaning.

You might think **Speak** is just a trick command. It doesn't have much practical use. There aren't many times when you want your dog to bark, yet barking is not only natural to your dog, your dog loves it. It is pleasurable. When nothing else is going on **Speak** is a great way to have some easy communication with your dog.

Walking, Riding, and Adventures

Walking your dog should always be a positive experience. Bathroom breaks and exercise can help meet more than physiological needs. When your dog goes out the door with you there are usually three possible purposes you could have in mind: walking your dog for a bathroom break; walking your dog for exercise or play; and/or taking your dog for a ride in the car.

It's a good idea to let your dog know which is about to happen. Rustling your car keys or saying something like, "Do you want to go for a ride?" are good clues for a mobile adventure, if they always precede the trip.

When it's time to walk your dog, try to

distinguish between bathroom breaks and the exercise/fun walk. The way to do this is to have a designated place that you routinely go to for bathroom breaks. Behind our house there's a patch of woods that provides a nice unused space with good natural composting for Chimo to use every day. I walk to a particular tree and let her have the full length of her leash to find her perfect spot on the surrounding ground. The only reason I ever take her there is for her bathroom breaks. That means, when she goes there, she knows exactly what's expected. After a little sniffing she usually goes right to work.

When I take her for an exercise/fun walk I always take her to her bathroom break area first. That way she's not so likely to do her business all over the neighborhood or at the park. The same applies when we're taking her for a ride in the car. That minimizes the need to do a cleanup at the destination.

To make this strategy work for you, establish a routine and stick with it. Even if you walk your dog in a more urban/suburban landscape and have to pick up after your dog every time, it's a good idea to follow this game plan. When you leave the house, you can go in one direction for bathroom breaks and then proceed in a different direction for exercise and fun. The payoff is when you're in a hurry or the weather is bad and you need your dog to do the deed without delay. If you have a well-defined bathroom area, your dog will get the message.

You can even use the **Go Ahead** command, explained elsewhere, to coax things along. **Go Ahead** can have the extra meaning of *Hurry up!*

Using commands in different contexts is a great way to expand their meanings and encourage more complex thinking. It also challenges your dog to solve the problem of understanding what you are trying to communicate. Your dog's vocabulary will become richer for it.

After you teach your dog to be comfortable home alone, you can also teach it to be a well-behaved rider. Plan some outings that you know will be fun adventures for your dog. Not every trip needs to be entertaining, but if enough of them are, your dog will develop a strong positive association with riding. You can mix things up, but have the general rule that if you know it is going to be a long boring trip in a hot car, your dog will probably be happier napping at home.

Striking a balance is the objective. Making sure your dog has a healthy attitude to your car will be beneficial when its time to go to the vet. A trip to the vet can be an upsetting experience for any dog. It can also make your dog fearful of entering your car, if that is its only riding experience. On the other hand, if the vet visit is a relatively rare experience compared to the many other happier times, your dog is more apt to stay calm and be better behaved.

Imagine your dog at the vet wondering if a fun adventure is about to begin. By the time it catches on the episode is over. To smooth the experience more follow it up with a romp at the park.

WALKING, RIDING, AND ADVENTURES

Hop Up and Hop Over

Now that you've taught your dog not to impulsively jump up on you, maybe we should also try to teach the opposite. Jumping up on you to reach your face comes natural to your dog, especially since you've been doing the same thing when you teach and show affection using face-to-face.

To invite or not to invite your dog to jump on you; that is the question. Invitation is the correct way to think about the **Hop Up** command. You need to make it clear that you're not granting *carte blanche* privileges. Personally, I don't mind my dog jumping up on occasion, as long as it's with my permission.

Hop Up is probably the easiest lesson you'll ever teach. Only work on this command if your dog is well behaved around guests and understands the **Down** command.

To teach **Hop Up** all you need to do is pat your chest or whatever part of your body that's within your dog's jumping range, while saying **Hop Up** with some friendly enthusiasm. If your dog doesn't respond immediately, I'll be amazed. You can always lift your dog's front paws to demonstrate the action. Use **Down** when you've had enough.

There are two good reasons for teaching **Hop Up**. First, it helps soften any lingering rejection your dog is apt to feel from being taught not to jump on you as a greeting. Second, it will lead to another handy command you can add to your dog's vocabulary.

Hop Over is great for directing your dog to go over some obstacle rather than crawling under it or going around it. A circus dog does a lot of **Hop Overs**. Your dog will have **Hop Over** occasions, too. For example, you'll probably want your dog to **Hop Over** some muck in the yard, rather than walk through it and track it in the house.

When you teach this command, set up a situation where **Hop Over** is easy and something your dog will probably choose to do anyway. Wave your arms to illustrate the move while you say **Hop Over** enthusiastically. If necessary, you can use a leash to give your dog the extra direction it might need.

Fortunately, dogs understand pointing and hand gestures. **Hop Up** and **Hop Over** are just two commands in a family of commands that involve the positioning of your dog. The others are **Get**, **Look Out**, **Get Back There**, **Get Over There**, **Stay**, and **Come Here**. When you have all of these in your command kit, you'll almost be able to parallel park your dog. Before you go overboard with these commands, please reserve them for times when you really need to help your dog. I hope you won't use them to turn your dog into a remote control toy for amusement purposes.

Look Out and Get

The related commands in this family have different meanings; however, they all have the general effect of sending your dog away from you. Since we don't want your dog to feel rejection unnecessarily, I recommend starting with **Look Out**.

Your dog wants to be included in whatever is going on with the family/pack. When you're sitting in your favorite chair reading or watching TV, I can picture your dog curled up at your feet. Yes, your dog wants to be close to you, but it also knows that whenever you stand up to go somewhere it will be alerted. It's difficult to

LOOK OUT AND GET

always tip-toe around your dog without being discovered. Dogs like to be underfoot.

Sooner or later being underfoot will cause a problem. You may be walking along and there's your dog blocking the way. This is the time to introduce **Look Out**. Use it as a warning. The first time you try out the command, you'll probably get a silly look. If so, gently bump into your dog while repeating it. Your dog will catch on quickly and come to take the warning seriously. If you want more practice, chase your dog around and say **Look Out**. Gently bump while repeating the command. Keep the tone of your voice friendly. You want your dog to think of it as word-to-the-wise advice.

Teaching **Look Out** first will help your dog understand that you aren't rejecting it when you introduce **Get** and the other commands that require your dog to move for no apparent reason. You want your dog to recognize that there's a sincere intent behind all these commands, so **Look Out** is the best place to start.

Look Out will also be helpful to you if your dog is overly protective of its space, such as around its food dish. When you need to cross through a danger zone, saying **Look Out** will tell your dog to stand down. It will make your dog less likely to feel threatened and allow you to pass without a problem. You can use the command in other situations, too. For example, let's say you're

LOOK OUT AND GET

cleaning up an area and you need your dog to move so you can sweep. Rather than chase your dog away with the broom while using a more harsh command like **Get**, take a cooperative tact and say **Look Out**.

Get simply means *Go Away!* I don't like using it, yet since there are times you'll really need your dog to immediately go away, you'll need to teach **Get** to your dog. It's also an important command because it's a building block for two other movement commands. Once your dog has learned the other **Get** commands, **Get** by itself won't seem like such a put down to your dog.

When you teach **Get**, use a sharp tone in your voice and point away in the direction you want it to go. The tone combined with the hand signal should give your dog the message. If it doesn't respond immediately, repeat and get a little angry. Dogs understand anger and can certainly express it themselves. Your dog will probably back down and retreat, especially if this is the first time you've directed any anger toward it.

When your dog responds and moves far enough away to satisfy you, cap it off with a quick low-key **Good Dog**. That will help de-escalate the situation. Make sure you don't confuse your dog into returning, though. If your dog starts to come back, repeat the **Get** command until it remains away.

LOOK OUT AND GET

You can toss in a **Stay** to clarify your intent, if necessary. Don't mix **Stay** with **Get** too often. **Get** means, *Go away to wherever you wish, as long as it's not here.* **Stay** freezes your dog, which isn't your intent. Be sure to keep your dog away so it doesn't think its a game. You want your dog to understand that **Get** also means *go away and stay away*.

Next, you can teach **Get Back There**. If you've been playing the biscuit tossing game with your dog, as I previously described, this command will take no time to teach. In the game your dog probably comes as close to you as possible to grab the treat with an easy catch. Before you toss it, say **Get Back There** and point in the direction behind your dog. Use a tone consistent with the game. There's no need to bark it just because **Get** is part of it. Don't toss the biscuit until your dog moves back. Repeat the command, if necessary. That's all there is to it. Use **Get Back There** every time before you toss a biscuit to your dog to reinforce the command. As your dog catches on, drop the hand signal and only use the voice command.

Your dog may make a sudden dash closer to you just before you make the toss. If that happens, do a pitcher's balk and repeat **Get Back There** to return your dog to the proper position. You may need to use **Stay** to prevent your dog from sneaking up again. Sending your dog back will add a degree of difficulty to the catch, but it also requires your dog to focus more. Without realizing it, your dog will learn what **Get Back There** means.

Teaching this way will associate positive experiences to **Get Back There**. By extension, whenever your dog hears **Get**, it won't feel as rejected. Don't confuse the two commands. Never use **Get Back There** when you mean, *go away and stay away*. They need to have distinct meanings. **Get Back There** means, *back up so something can happen*. **Get Back There** has a short-lived meaning. When your dog responds to **Get Back There**, within moments your dog is allowed to reunite with you or do whatever it wants. There's no rejection or *stay away* involved.

The final **Get** command is **Get Over There**. This requires your dog to check with you for hand signals, as you'll be pointing in a particular direction. At first your dog will probably confuse **Get Over There** with **Get Back There**, which also began with a hand gesture. **Get Over There** means *notice where I'm pointing and go in that direction*. **Get Back There** means, *back up in that specific direction away from me*. A good way to teach this one is to teach **Look** as a separate command first.

By now you've already established the full meaning of **Look Out** to be something like *heads up and move because you're about to bumped*.

Set up a situation where your dog is hunting for something and you know where it's. Make sure you're standing away from your dog. If your dog is searching in the wrong area and you point to the correct location while saying **Get Over There**, your dog may not notice you. Instead, say **Look**. Your dog will probably think **Look Out** and notice you, expecting it will have to move to avoid you or something else. Now that you've grabbed your dog's attention, say **Get Over There** with the appropriate pointing. Eventually your dog will understand that it needs to look for a hand signal whenever it hears **Get Over There**. At that point **Look** will become unnecessary part of the routine. The helpfulness of your **Get Over There** pointing clue is what solidifies the command.

Without much effort you've also taught your dog the **Look** command. You won't need it to move your dog in a particular direction; you'll use it in other situations instead. **Look** doesn't necessarily mean *notice me*; it just means *look*. It's much closer to **What is it?** Use **What is it?** when you want your dog to scan its senses and respond to something obvious. A good way to use **Look** is in close range situations when you're pointing at something that your dog would miss entirely without the hand gestures. **Look** will urge your dog to use its eyesight. **What is it?** will stimulate hearing. The distinctions are subtle, and you'll be fine if you simply use one or the other. I favor using both because they're so easy to teach, and creating the distinction is a good way to challenge your dog's thinking ability.

Get Back There and **Get Over There** work well for guiding your dog to find a hidden tennis ball, yet there are many tricky situations where these commands can help you navigate your dog to safety. You might find your dog is confused about how to get around something or unsure about how to position itself to navigate unfamiliar territory. Climbing into a boat or untangling its leash are just two examples.

With these and other commands in combination you can in effect parallel park your dog. If you employ them in meaningful situations, your dog will want you to use them. Your dog should know that you are its helpful friend and not a puppet master. Your dog can tell when you make it perform pointless tricks. Taught properly and used properly, your dog will eagerly listen to your commands to help it solve problems and stay safe and happy.

Let's Go and Go Ahead

The **Let's Go** and **Go Ahead** commands are cousins to the **Get** commands and are easy to teach. They make handy additions to your dog's vocabulary.

Let's Go is a phrase that you can use to alert your dog that something is happening and it should come along. Sometimes your dog is peacefully relaxing or playing in another room unsuspecting that it's time for a walk or an adventure. Use **Let's Go** to get your dog to hurry up and join the parade. This is distinct from **Come Here**, which is used to bring your dog to a specific spot — you. **Let's Go** informs your dog that an activity is about to take place and that it needs to get into the flow.

When your dog understands **Let's Go**, you can then start using **Go Ahead** to prompt your dog to proceed in front of you. Point and say **Go Ahead** and your dog will grasp the meaning quickly. *Go* is the key sound that links the two commands and makes **Go Ahead** easy to teach.

It may take some repetition to lock it into your dog's vocabulary. Once that happens, it can be used in many other situations, even if you won't be following. For example, you can use it to prompt your dog to go up or down stairs, as you'll see with the **Upstairs** command. Or, use it in any situation where your dog might be hesitating to do something. Let's say you take your dog swimming and your dog is balking at jumping into the water. The **Go Ahead** command can make the difference. There are dozens of everyday situations where you'll want to use **Go Ahead** to coax your dog.

Drop It, Pick It Up, Bring It Here, and Get It

Dogs can be sensitive when it comes to their mouths. They're often particular about what they're willing to pick up. There are dogs that will go crazy over a tennis ball and rip a cloth toy apart, but won't touch something made of rubber or plastic. Other dogs will grab anything. Puppies are particularly indiscriminate. As you go through these commands, respect your dog's sensitivities.

Your dog should learn **Drop It** as a puppy. Chewing on the wrong object will quickly earn a **No** or a **Bad Dog**. Before relying on either of these commands, try to teach **Drop It**. Combine it with a menacing tone and your dog will get the idea quickly and comply. If so, your dog deserves some praise instead of further criticism. That will get your dog's attention and help keep things calm for the follow up step.

Hold the item and point to it. Use the **No** command in combination with **Drop It**. **Bad Dog** should be unnecessary. Eventually your dog will get the idea. At first **Drop It** will mean *I must eject whatever is in my mouth.*

Learning this command is important to the health and safety of your dog. If you catch your dog with a putrid animal or piece of harmful trash in its mouth, you'll want your dog to give it up immediately.

Drop It can also be used to prevent your dog from grabbing something it shouldn't. If it starts sniffing at your food, **Drop It** will tell your dog not to bother. If you happen to catch your dog approaching a wild animal, such as a skunk or porcupine, you'll be glad that your dog understands **Drop It** and will follow your instructions. In these instances the specific meaning of **Drop It** is *don't put it in my mouth in the first place.* This combination of meanings eject and avoid doesn't conform to the literal English meaning of **Drop It**. Of course, literal meanings matter nothing to your dog, so having two separate commands to cover these simple concepts is unnecessary.

The opposite command is **Pick It Up**. **Pick**

It Up can be taught in a few different ways. If you do the biscuit toss game, add a few warm up arm movements before the actual toss. Repeat **Pick It Up** with each swing of your arm. Another way to teach **Pick It Up** is to say it over and over while your dog is eating. Not everything your dog picks up with this command is meant to be chewed or swallowed. Once you think your dog grasps the concept, test it by pointing to a favorite toy and say **Pick It Up**. If your dog doesn't respond, get the toy and give it to your dog. If your dog accepts it, repeat the command with a nice serving of praise and affection.

Once your dog is past the chewing stage, you can add **Bring It Here** to the mix as in **Pick It Up** and **Bring It Here**. Be sure to point to the object you want. The **Bring It Here** part should have the same ring as **Come Here**. Some of the methods you used to teach **Come Here** can be applied to this lesson. If you speak slowly and clearly to your dog, you can try combining the commands in this way: **Pick It Up Bring It Here Come Here Bring It Here**. Inserting the familiar **Come Here** command can clarify the **Bring It Here** expectation. Once your dog becomes familiar with **Pick It Up** and **Bring It Here**, you can phase out **Come Here**. Make sure that **Pick It Up** and **Bring It Here** has a meaning separate from **Come Here**. **Pick It Up** and **Bring It Here** has the added meaning of *don't come here with an* *empty mouth.*

Pick It Up and **Bring It Here** can be used as a jumping off point to teach object specific commands.

Put your slippers in the room and point to them, saying **Pick It Up** and **Bring It Here**. After a few successes, add **Slippers** to the command mix so you have **Pick It Up Slippers Bring It Here**. Don't say, "Pick up the slippers and bring them here". That has too many unfamiliar sounds. It will be confusing because your dog doesn't understand English syntax and therefore can't unpack all the meanings. As your dog performs the task and is rewarded, start gradually dropping words until you get down to the one word command, **Slippers**. You'll want that to mean *go find the slippers and bring them to me*. Using the simple word **Slippers** is enough.

Once your dog is performing properly, move your slippers farther and farther away while practicing the command. Eventually put them in the spot they're normally kept, such as in your closet or by your bed. You'll want to teach this in gradual steps because your dog is apt to think you want whatever object is in the location where the lesson began. Eventually you can drop the pointing and your dog will run off to find your slippers and bring them to you.

There are dogs trained to identify and fetch hundreds of items with commands like this.

DROP IT, PICK IT UP, BRING IT HERE, AND GET IT

Teaching your dog to get your slippers falls into the category of tricks, so I no longer teach my dogs to get my slippers and other objects. On the other hand, you may have a specific need for your dog to fetch something that's necessary to improve your life. If so, I'm all in favor of teaching your dog using this technique. There are thousands of dogs who perform amazing assisted living tasks every day. They are true heroes.

Regardless of what you decide to do, this technique demonstrates how easy it's to take simple commands and use them in combinations to create new commands with different meanings.

Before moving on let's take this one step further. Dogs love to play keep-away. Unfortunately, when you're trying to teach your dog to fetch the tennis ball for fun and exercise, keep-away often creeps into the game; however, if you use **Pick It Up** and **Bring It Here** along with **Drop It**, you can teach your dog proper tennis ball etiquette. Once you dog becomes a well-behaved playmate, stop barking those commands and insert something new, **Get It**. As you throw the ball and your dog runs off, repeat **Get It** excitedly a few times.

Be careful when you use **Get It** in other situations. You may inadvertently be teaching your dog **Sic 'Em**. Dogs aren't deliberately taught **Sic 'Em** much anymore because it's potentially dangerous to people and other animals. **Sic 'Em** traditionally means attack and kill. You don't want your dog attacking small children in the neighborhood.

I've used **Get It** to excite Chimo into chasing squirrels for some cheap exercise. She's too old to catch them anymore, so it's really just a game to keep her senses sharp. If your dog is a better hunter, act accordingly.

All dogs do have an attack and kill instinct simmering below the surface. If your dog is relatively tame like Chimo, you won't have a problem. Tame dogs still like to play attack and kill in a harmless way. Chasing the tennis ball is your dog's pretend play version of hunting small animals. **Get It** can also be used at home to pique your dog's interest in a new squeaky toy.

Add **Get It** to the **Get** family of commands.

Upstairs

The **Upstairs** command must be among the two or three easiest ones to teach, yet it will amaze your friends when they see it in action. It does have practical value, so it's not exactly a trick. It also illustrates how easily you can invent new commands using the regular behavior of your dog with a little help from commands already in your dog's vocabulary.

If you have stairs in your house that you trek regularly with your dog, say **Upstairs** over and over as you climb them. When you get to the top, heap some praise and affection on your dog. At first your dog won't understand why it's getting the reward, but that's okay. After it's heard **Upstairs** a few dozen times, stand at the bottom, point up, say **Upstairs**, and see what your dog does. Chances are your dog will figure it out right away and proceed to the top while you stay where you are. When your dog gets to the top, rush up and give the usual reward. If your dog doesn't respond, you can try adding **Go Ahead**, assuming that's already a part of its vocabulary. If that doesn't work, go upstairs with your dog repeating **Upstairs** as you did previously. With enough repetition your dog is sure to understand and perform as expected.

When **Upstairs** is learned, test your dog by standing a few feet away from the bottom of the stairs while you point and issue the command. As you continue to practice, stand farther and farther away from the stairs. Eventually you'll be able to sit in another room and you won't need to point.

Repeating **Upstairs** whenever you go upstairs is the crucial first step. Take your time with that part and the rest will go amazingly fast.

I get asked, "What about downstairs?" It's unnecessary to create a separate command. If you use **Upstairs** for both directions, your dog will have no problem understanding. Up and down mean nothing to your dog. Your dog will understand the **Upstairs** command to mean *get on the stairs and travel*. Your dog will associate it with the place. The direction will be obvious.

I rarely use this command. My boys use it when the plan is for Chimo to sleep in their room. If you train your dog to fetch something for you, as in the **Slippers** command, and if the object is upstairs, the **Upstairs** command can be a helpful hint to a confused dog.

Whispering

The goal of everything so far is to show you how to teach the important commands in a way that will also fulfill your dog's highest needs, especially nature, curiosity, spontaneity, problem-solving, and communication. The purpose is to help you connect with your dog's heart to have a deeper companionship relationship. To help make that possible, the lessons are designed to keep things calm between you and your dog. Instinctively, your dog will be drawn closer to you when you demonstrate kindness and friendship. Yelling at your dog and using harsh training methods might make your dog obey, but it won't enhance its happiness and it won't build a bridge to your dog's heart. To feel fulfilled, your dog comes to you with a desire to be involved in the details of your world.

Even if your dog was abused before you brought it home, it's never too late for you to say *hello in there* and demonstrate that you want to be a true companion.

As these techniques begin to work and your dog responds, be sure to spend plenty of both raucous playtime and quiet nap time with your dog without the burden of lessons. It's important to have the ready attention of your dog that naturally flows from plain old bonding. The more your dog is engaged in your world, the more it will look for new things to learn on its own.

When all the pieces fit together and you feel your dog is immersed in your life, try testing your dog's awareness. Call your dog over and run through a few simple commands in a soft voice. If your dog can respond just as well when hearing whispered commands, congratulations! You've achieved a terrific milestone. You'll know that your dog genuinely honors your words and values their meanings.

When you talk in a soft voice, you'll also be teaching your dog to become an excellent listener. By carefully listening and observing your world, your dog will become a prodigious learner. You really can make that happen.

The flip side is that your dog will expect

the same from you. If you become a good listener and respond to what your dog is trying to communicate, your dog will have the confidence to be more spontaneous with you. You should welcome all this and use it to help your dog have, as much as possible, a co-equal position alongside you and the other members of your family/pack.

The Journey

Dogs have been accepted into human society for thousands of years. Companionship has always been important, but the roles allocated to dogs have been primarily as helpers and workers. At first their duties were to hunt and protect. Their keen sense of smell was an important asset when tracking prey. Back at the camp they could sense predators lurking about and provide an early warning. Later, as other animals were domesticated, dogs learned to herd. Before the introduction of horses, Native Americans even used dogs as pack animals. Wherever life was most tenuous, the decision to keep a dog depended primarily on its ability to support human survival.

For centuries the beating and mistreatment of dogs was an accepted method for controlling their behavior. The methodical subjugation of dogs continued into the twentieth century. Not so long ago the expression *A woman, a dog, and a walnut tree; the more you beat 'em, the better they be* was still being used as an accepted proverb. [1929 E. Linklater Poet's Pub xii.]

Fortunately, as family dogs became more common with suburbanization, their treatment improved. By the 1960s most dogs still lived entirely outdoors and were kept mainly for protection and as playmates for young children.

Over the past forty years things have really changed. These days, in the United States, more and more dogs live inside, and their status in the family circle has risen significantly. In spite of this special proximity, dogs are too often adopted for amusement with little regard for their individual fulfillment.

Today the evidence showing that dogs are thinking, feeling beings like we are is overwhelming. We must therefore accept that every dog also has a complex set of needs. It's your duty to care for your dog's unique emotional and mental life. Your dog depends on you for that support to fulfill its highest needs.

The compassion I'm sure you feel for your dog will make this an enjoyable and gratifying mission. Throughout its life you'll be rewarded every day with the constant love and gratitude flowing from the heart of your dog.

There's a new movement calling for greater altruism in the way we treat all animals. The logical implication for the family dog is a renewed focus on its happiness.

No one knows for sure if dogs have self-awareness. Do they feel oppressed or enslaved when they're forced into lives of compulsory work? Is freedom a concept they can understand the way we do? Someday we may know the answers with certainty. Regardless, we've learned to have a greater concern for their wellbeing and happiness. In the process we've discovered the benefits that come with deeper levels of companionship.

This is my journey. When I was a small child a collie named Rusty was the first dog I knew. Rusty was never chained and never knew a leash. He lived entirely outdoors. He was free to roam the woods and come home to romp with me. At the sound of a bell he would run to the door for his daily can of Alpo. He slept in his dog house and never rode in the car except for occasional trips to the vet. To me, in my limited way of understanding the world, he was simply a lovable and mysterious playmate.

Since then I've always had one or more dogs. My appreciation of their complex lives has grown over the years. Today Chimo is nearly equal to any of my children within our family circle. All her needs from physiological to fulfillment are being met. She extends her heart to us every day and we reciprocate with our offer of lifelong companionship.

This book is a summary of what I've learned. It's incomplete because every dog is unique. You'll find so much more about your dog on your own. The lessons I explain are intended as a guide to help you launch a deeper relationship with your dog. I've had a unique experience with each of my dogs. You should expect the same.

This book gives you a blueprint to find and open doors most people don't realize exist. As you walk through those doors, you'll discover things that will take you and your dog to new places. There's so much more you'll need to invent along the way. Your journey will have many exciting twists and turns. All I can promise is that each moment of happiness you share will bring you closer to the heart of your dog.

Index

A

alpha-male dog 22–23
A Theory of Human Motivation 26

B

Bad Dog 77–82, 103–104
barking 18, 57, 82, 107
Buck 1, 22

C

Call of the Wild 22
chewing 51–52, 66, 103, 105
children 5, 7, 11, 24, 26, 36–37, 43, 53, 116
Chimo 8, 36, 42, 49, 77, 80, 87, 108, 111, 117
Come Here 58–65, 69, 79, 105
communication 3, 6, 29, 31, 36–38, 39, 43, 50, 52, 75, 85, 112, 114
confidence 5, 23, 29, 50, 65, 68, 76, 77, 81, 114
confusion 5, 46, 52, 72, 106, 111
crate training 45–50
curiosity 6, 17, 31, 32–33, 53, 112

D

dogness 9, 10–38, 20
dog ownership 7–38
dominance and submission 17, 22, 22–24, 39, 42
Down 55–57, 92
Drop It 103

INDEX

E

eye contact and staring 18–20, 39, 75

F

face-to-face 19, 40, 42, 44, 46, 51, 59, 60, 64, 70, 77, 91
family/pack 8, 13, 16, 24, 25, 28, 29, 32, 39, 43, 48, 50, 58, 82, 83, 94, 114
fulfillment 3, 6, 7, 31–38, 66, 113, 116, 118

G

games 34–35, 97–98, 100, 105–108
Get 95–99, 101
Get Back There 97–99
Get Over There 98–99
Go Ahead 88, 101–103, 110
Good Dog 20, 77–82, 96

H

hand signals 21, 93
Hierarchy of Canine Familiaris Needs 26, 28, 31
Hierarchy of Needs 26, 27, 31
Hop Over 92–93
Hop Up 91–93
housebreaking 25, 45–50, 51, 60

I

imagination 3, 12–14
independent learner 3, 6, 36, 113
intelligence 1, 13–14, 20, 31
It's Alright 76

J

jealousy 17, 57
jumping 54–57, 91

K

knowing its name 58–59

120

INDEX

L

Lassie 1
leash 32, 59, 61, 63, 87, 93, 100, 117
Let's Go 101–103
licking 41–42
Lie Down 71
London, Jack 22
Look Out 94–95, 98–99

M

Maslow, Abraham 26–27
MRI and dogs 30
mutual respect 29, 62, 65, 81

N

nature 31–32, 112
No 51–53, 55, 103–104

O

obedience and obedience training 2, 25

P

parent/leader 24–26, 61, 66
Pavlov, Ivan 29
pet 7–8
physiological needs 3, 5–6, 26–27, 66, 86, 118
Pick It Up 104–108
Poor Dog 74–76
problem solving 5, 31, 34–35, 65, 100, 112
puppies 4, 6, 7, 16, 32, 39, 41, 45–50, 52, 57, 66–67, 103

Q

Quiet 82

R

riding 86–90
Right Now 63–65
Rin Tin Tin 1

INDEX

robot dog 2, 63
Rusty 117

S

safety needs 26, 28
self-awareness 30–31, 117
self-esteem 5, 29
separation anxiety 66–71
Sic 'Em 107
Sit 71
Slippers 106–107, 111
spontaneity 31, 33–34, 112, 114
Stay 69–71, 97

T

treats 43, 97–98
tricks 2, 72, 84, 100, 106–107

U

Upstairs 102, 109–112

V

vocabulary 3, 5, 6, 36–38, 52, 64, 75, 76, 84, 92, 101, 102, 109, 110

W

walking 86–90
What is it? 53, 99
whispering 112
wolves 6, 14, 15, 18, 19, 22–24, 49, 66

www.ingramcontent.com/pod-product-compliance
Lightning Source LLC
Chambersburg PA
CBHW071708040426
42446CB00011B/1961